WHAT IS THE TRINITY?

IS VOLUME

17

OF THE

Twentieth Century Encyclopedia of Catholicism

UNDER SECTION

II

THE BASIC TRUTHS

IT IS ALSO THE

11TH

VOLUME IN ORDER OF PUBLICATION

Edited by HENRI DANIEL-ROPS *of the Académie Française*

WHAT IS THE TRINITY?

By BERNARD PIAULT

Translated from the French by ROSEMARY HAUGHTON

HAWTHORN BOOKS · PUBLISHERS · *New York*

© 1959 by Hawthorn Books, Inc., 70 Fifth Avenue, New York City
11. Copyright under International and Pan-American Copyright Con-
ventions. All rights reserved, including the right to reproduce this
book, or portions thereof, in any form, except for the inclusion of
brief quotations in a review. This book was manufactured in the
United States of America and published simultaneously in Canada by
McClelland & Stewart, Ltd., 25 Hollinger Road, Toronto 16. Original
French edition, *Le mystère du Dieu vivant, Un et Trine* © F. Brouty,
J. Fayard et Cie, 1956. The Library of Congress has catalogued
The Twentieth Century Encyclopedia of Catholicism under card num-
ber 58-14327.

First Edition, February, 1959

NIHIL OBSTAT

Hubertus Richards, S.T.L., L.S.S.

Censor Deputatus

IMPRIMATUR

E. Morrogh Bernard

Vicarius Generalis

Westmonasterii, die XII NOVEMBRIS MCMLVIII

The Library of Congress has catalogued this publication as follows:

Piault, Bernard.
    What is the Trinity? [1st ed.] New York, Hawthorn Books [1959]

    156 p. 21 cm. (The Twentieth century encyclopedia of Catholicism, v. 17.
Section 2: The basic truths)

    Translation of Le mystère du Dieu vivant, un et trine.
Bibliography: p. 156.

    1. Trinity—History of doctrines. 2. Creeds.   I. Title.   (Series: The
Twentieth century encyclopedia of Catholicism, v. 17)

BT109.P513   231   58–11595

CONTENTS

CONTENTS

PART II: THE CHRISTIAN CREEDS

PART III: BELIEVING, KNOWING AND LIVING

INTRODUCTION

All things come from him,
All things exist through him,
All things live by him;
To him be glory for ever.

*(Fifth antiphon at Vespers on the
feast of the Blessed Trinity.)*

In his booklet on examination of conscience Fr Lebret suggests that we include in our self-examination the fault of "never meditating on the Trinity". Nothing is easier than for the Christian to answer him, the theologians and parish priests, "Examine your consciences yourselves; do you ever talk to the faithful about the Trinity?"

It is possible that these are both sins of our time. The Blessed Trinity is seldom preached from the Christian pulpit. The only things that are written about it are learned studies on special points for which theologians need a very strong lens to see them clearly. These works are necessary for the honour of learning and of the Church, and certainly the theologian also draws spiritual food from them to help him to the contemplation of God; for it is enthralling to live again the unfolding drama of faith through the eyes of past generations. Yet the Christian who cannot be a specialist on these questions, because other work claims his attention, does, nevertheless, need to know the Three-in-One in order the better to live in him.

It is necessary to set before him food which is suitable, not for a professor, but simply for a hungry adult. The Mystery of God must not remain hidden in books for specialists or the world will die of hunger; perhaps it is already doing so for lack of this food.

It is not that people do not know the articles of their faith: we all know the Apostles' Creed. But what Christian of today as he recites it feels the fervour that brought his brothers of the first centuries to their feet, alert to withstand the onslaught of heresy? That fervour was working also in the catechumens as they went down into the baptismal water where they would lovingly proclaim their devotion to God, Father, Son and Holy Spirit.

The purpose of this book is to supply a lack in the means available to the Christian who wants to widen his religious knowledge. In doing this I would like to make people realize the urgency of a better understanding of the Trinity in our age, even of the need to contemplate its mystery. To be overcome with wonder before this God who reveals himself to man, before the life of God himself, that life which he possesses as Three-in-One, that life which he freely gives to us; to find in contemplation of this mystery the source of all spiritual life and the mainspring of all action: it is to this goal that I should like to help all who read these pages.

A few preliminary remarks may make this aim more understandable. They will show clearly the great importance of reflecting on the mystery.

A Christian is not merely someone who believes in God, he is someone who believes in a God who is Father, Son, and Holy Spirit. It is this that distinguishes him from the pagan philosophers who admitted the existence of God but to whom the revelation of one God in Three Persons would have seemed merely a return to polytheism, a belief in a number of Gods. Their painstaking philosophical speculations had led them to one sole God but not as far as the Trinity.

Do we realize sufficiently that this is also what separates Christians from the Jewish nation, from Israel which was once God's chosen people? The fundamental question which divides us is none other than that of the unity and trinity of God. The problem for Israel is how to admit that Jesus can be God without endangering their faith in the one God: Yahweh and

Jesus would make two gods, the Holy Spirit would make a third, and the divine unity would be destroyed. Islam sees the problem in the same terms: our Trinity is horrible to them. So it becomes clear—and it has been so from the first—that a man is a Christian when he believes that the one God lives in Three Persons.

On the other hand—and surely this gives us ground to hope for a fruitful development of ideas with our separated brethren —all Christians share this faith in the Trinity. All Christians know the cross, the instrument by which the Son of God accomplished the redemption of the world. They know that God the Son died for them in obedience to the will of God the Father (Rom. 8. 3 and 32). All of them, when they trace on themselves the sign of their redemption, also devoutly name the three Persons by whom they are saved. All Christians, even though separated, remain united by their faith in the Trinity, faith that united them from the very beginning in the midst of persecution. The terrible wounds which they inflicted on each other on this account in the ninth, thirteenth and fifteenth centuries never entirely separated them. It was more a matter of mutual incomprehension than of fundamental disagreement. If ever a Christian dared to question the divinity of one of the three Persons, from that very moment he would lose the right to belong to any Christian denomination. The mystery of the Blessed Trinity is, therefore, the characteristic Christian mystery, and it shares this distinction with the mystery of the redemptive incarnation: in history they are inseparable.

Yet it is even more than this, it is the preeminent mystery. There is no doubt that people of our age long to turn towards Christ, towards his Church and his sacraments, and who can blame them, seeing how sickly they have grown from neglect of them? A man must die of thirst if he remains far from the giver of living water (John 4. 14) who pours it out so lavishly on his Church (John 7. 37–9). Let us therefore turn to the Mystery of Christ and his sacraments, to the liturgy of the Church.

At the same time we must not allow the vital theology of the Incarnate Word to make us forget the other aspect of revelation, that which extends even to the inner life of God himself. God willed to tell us about himself; clearly, then, it is important for us to know him. We must believe the words of Jesus: "Eternal life is knowing thee, who art the only true God, and Jesus Christ whom thou hast sent" (John 17. 3). Christ, then, bids us turn not only to his revelation of himself (John 1. 18), but also towards the source from which he comes and to which he has returned for our sakes (John 14. 2).

Ignatius, the aged bishop of Antioch, said at the beginning of the second century, at the very moment when he was seeking for Jesus so that he might imitate him in his martyrdom: "I hear a voice that says to me 'Come to the Father'" (*Epistle to the Romans*, 7. 2). It was the voice of the Holy Spirit that whispered in his ear inviting him to forsake with good cheer this mortal life and the pleasures it brings, for none of them can compare with the joy that the Father has prepared for those who love him (1 Cor. 2. 9). If Jesus is the way, the Father is the goal, and Jesus has given us his Spirit so that we may know how to reach it (John 16. 13–14).

Eternal life is to know the Father, the Son, and the Holy Spirit and, as St John tells us, eternal Life begins even here on earth. At baptism we receive a pledge of it: we are reborn for eternity (John 3. 3–5), we are introduced into the friendship of the Three-in-One. It would be very odd if, called to a life of such intimacy with God, Christians never concerned themselves about it. Psichari trembled with love when he reflected that he was writing in the presence of the Trinity. We also must tremble with love and joy when, at the invitation of Jesus, our Bridegroom, we enter into the nuptial chamber of the Scriptures, when we live again with the apostles, with Christians of all the centuries of our Faith, the mystery of God: Father, Son, and Holy Spirit, in whom all things exist and from whom all things come. The love of God will work this miracle: two wholly dissimilar beings, the infinite God and we his creatures, will achieve that union for which Jesus prayed (John 17. 21). Then, here on earth, our eternal life will begin, the three Persons will reproduce in us their own inner relationship, and we shall know it. May this knowledge enable us to give them greater glory: when all is said it is this which is the gift of the Spirit.

> Per te sciamus da Patrem
> Noscamus atque Filium
> Teque utriusque Spiritum
> Credamus omni tempore.[1]

[1] Through thee may we the Father know,
Through thee the eternal Son
And thee the Spirit of them both
Thrice blessed Three in One.

PART I

SEARCHING THE SCRIPTURES[1]

"Then he enlightened their minds to make them
understand the Scriptures" (Luke 24. 45).

The mystery of the blessed Trinity was only revealed by Jesus.
All the same, before beginning to read the New Testament, it
is a good thing to examine the revelation that God made to
the Jewish people in the Old Testament. We shall not find in it
a lesson on the Trinity—there is none—but a preparation for
the revelation of the mystery. We shall find in it the living God,
at once remote from and yet close to mankind; the mysterious
Being whose actions transcend thought, who yet invites man to
consider his personal life and his method of working in the
world.

[1] This first part of the book needs to be read with a Bible open at
one's side. The Knox version of the Bible is used throughout this book.

CHAPTER I

THE OLD TESTAMENT AND THE LIVING GOD

THE DIVINE TUTELAGE

Only gradually has God revealed the mystery of his own being. This preparatory statement is necessary for an understanding of the whole of his revelation. God first established monotheism on firm foundations,[1] as the basic dogma[2] that bound Israel to the one God, Yahweh. It was necessary at all costs to purify the religious ideas of the Jews, endangered as they were by the surrounding polytheism. To have revealed the mystery of the Trinity at that time would have been to threaten the purity of Israel's religion: the Jews would certainly have come to worship three gods.

At the same time God needed to prepare souls to receive one day the word of Christ and his apostles proclaiming that Yahweh was one God in whom existed a trinity of Persons. It is possible to see how, under the guidance of the Holy Spirit who inspired the leading religious figures of Israel, ideas developed which would one day enable those who belonged to the "true Israel" to receive with ready and eager hearts the

[1] The doctrine which teaches the existence of one sole God. (See also Volumes 15 and 16 of this series.)

[2] A dogma: a truth contained in Scripture and in the teaching of tradition, and guaranteed as such by the authority of the Church. (Definition of the Vatican Council.) See Volume 4 in this series.

message that Jesus brought concerning the Three-in-One. We can examine a few of these ideas:

The Old Testament does not tell us that there is a Father in God, a Person distinct from the other two persons; it tells us that God is a father, but without disclosing the depths of his fatherhood. Yet Israel was perfectly conscious of a metaphorical fatherhood in God, a metaphor justified not by physical generation but by a free choice governed by love.

Israel knew itself the People of God, knew also that it was the "son of Yahweh,"[3] his only son, "his first-born" (Exod. 4. 22).[4] The prophet Osee describes the fatherly feelings that show his love (11. 1–4).

The very names of the Israelites show this deep conviction that Yahweh is a father. For instance, *Abiyya*, "my father is Yahweh" (1 Paral. 7. 18), *Abitob*, "my father is goodness" (1 Paral. 8. 11); *Abiezer*, "my father is my help" (Jos. 17. 2). Yahweh is father of a people, but also the father of the righteous. The impious man, he who does not keep the law of Yahweh, cannot be his son. The righteous man, on the contrary, has God for his father, he is "the son of God" and he knows it:

> He envies the just their future happiness,
> boasts of a divine parentage.
> Put we his claims, then, to the proof;
> let experience show what end awaits him.
> If to be just is to be God's son indeed,
> then God will take up his cause,
> will save him from the power of his enemies.
>
> (Wisdom 2. 11–18)[5]

But God himself calls the righteous his sons:
"Know, then, my children . . ." (Ps. 33. 12).[6]
He is their shepherd and his house is their house (Ps. 23 and 41).

---

[3] Yahweh, the divine name revealed to Moses (Exod. 3. 14) and which means, in the scriptural tradition, "He who is".
[4] See also Deut. 14. 1; Isaias 63. 16; 64. 7; Jer. 3. 19; 31. 20.
[5] See also Ps. 72. 28 and 102. 13–14.
[6] Same form of address in Prov. 8. 32–33.

Also supremely righteous is the Messias, preeminent among the sons of God. Yahweh thus names him, and he himself lays claim to a sonship, which gives him rights over the whole earth:

To me he has given a kingly throne upon mount Sion,
his sanctuary, there to proclaim his edict,
how he told me, Thou art my son, I have begotten thee this day.

(Ps. 2. 6–7)

He is to be born of a woman of acknowledged virginity (Isaias 7. 14). The prophet sees him as endowed with extraordinary prerogatives: he is to be strong, eternal, a bringer of peace (Isaias 9. 6). The spirit of Yahweh will rest upon him, with all his gifts (Isaias 2. 1–5).

It is clear that the divine sonship of the Messias does not differ from that of other just men; but it is more perfect of its kind, in that it emphasizes the special love of Yahweh for the one whom he has raised up. Yahweh's choice of him is the source of the Messias' moral qualities. Nowadays we would say that his relationship with Yahweh was one of sonship through grace. In fact, this characteristic is clearly underlined by the prophet Daniel (7. 13). The prophet sees the Messias coming on the clouds of heaven. He appears as a "son of man" in spite of the altogether singular power and transcendence that surround him with a halo of mystery, placing him among divine beings. But for the Israelite of the time of Isaias or Daniel, as well as from the eighth to the second century before Christ, the Messias was not the son of God in the sense that we know that Jesus is. The monotheism of Israel was fiercely opposed to such a concept. The idea of an internal fecundity in God would have made no sense to an Israelite.

THE INTERMEDIARIES

It is quite clear that the Messias, because he was to be the "son of Yahweh", was to have a part to play in the community of Israel. Because of his presence in its heart, as its centre and its king, Israel was to become precisely a messianic community, that is, the ideal people willed by God and guided by him. Isaias had foretold it:

Ever wider shall his dominion spread, endlessly at peace;
he will sit on David's kingly throne, to give it lasting foundations
of justice, and right; so tenderly he loves us, the Lord of hosts.
(Isaias 9. 7)

About three centuries later in a prophetic vision a new prophet described the fulfilment of what was anticipated by this oracle. The exile in Babylon would come to an end, the people would enjoy the happy days of the return. Isaias 60, in a magnificent panorama that the Church gives us to read every year on the feast of the Epiphany—the feast on which she celebrates in particular this youthful royalty of the Son of God— and Isaias 66. 18–24, show us the perfect messianic kingdom. All peoples would come before Yahweh to adore him, all the nations would be gathered together, there would be a new heaven and a new earth, for the time would have come when the Messias, the peace-maker, would reign. The Messias was, precisely, an intermediary between God and men, one who was sent at the time ordained by Yahweh. Michaeas (5. 1–2) had foretold the place of his birth and Daniel had foreseen his coming one day on the clouds of heaven to reign over an empire that should never be destroyed (Dan. 7. 13–14). And there were other envoys whose function it was equally to continue Yahweh's work among men. Of this kind were the Angel of the Lord, Wisdom, the Word, the Spirit. The more remote and mysterious God became, all the more living did he seem, all the more did he draw near through his messengers.

THE ANGEL OF THE LORD

The Angel of the Lord is a mysterious person who speaks in the name of God whose messenger he is. In Genesis (16. 9–10) he appears to Agar, Abraham's servant, telling her to go back to Sarai, and tell her on Yahweh's behalf, that she, Agar, is to be the mother of a great race. In the book of Judges (13. 3) the Angel of the Lord comes to the wife of Manue, who was barren, and tells her also that she will have a child, Samson. At the beginning of the New Testament the Angel Gabriel is sent by God to Zachary with a similar message: John the Baptist is to be born to Elizabeth who had been barren (Luke 1. 2). He comes to the Virgin Mary who, in her turn, learns from him that despite her virginity Jesus will be born of her (Luke 1. 26). Through him many other messages also are made known, such an assurance of victory in war (Judges 6. 7; 2. 12; Isaias 37. 36).

In some other accounts, usually older ones which historical scholarship and criticism attributes to the document known as "J", or "Yahwist",[7] drawn up about a thousand years before Christ, it was God himself who appeared and spoke. This can be seen in Genesis 18. Yahweh comes to Abraham and his wife Sarai and speaks to them, yet in the second verse Yahweh becomes three men standing before Abraham. In this case then, there are intermediaries, the three men are the ambassadors of Yahweh. In the Exodus the traditions are mixed. In the theophany[8] of the burning bush it is the Angel of the Lord who first makes his presence known (Exod. 3. 2), but from the sixth verse onwards it is Yahweh himself who speaks.

From these few remarks it is possible to draw the following conclusions: the first biblical accounts did not scruple to describe God as appearing in person, nor to show him working personally among men. Read the second account of the creation: Yahweh forms man from the slime of the earth (Gen. 2. 7). Further on we see him walking in Paradise, in Eden, in the cool of the evening (3. 8). But to a later age it seemed that it was not proper for God to come in person. In the first chapter of Genesis, which contains a later account of the creation, God acts by his word alone. But the angels were also to assume considerable importance. As the word itself shows in Hebrew and Greek, angel means "one who is sent". Angels are the legates and ambassadors of Yahweh. When, according to tradition, seventy Greek scholars in the second century B.C. made the

---

[7] So named because in it God is called Yahweh. See also Vols. 60, 63 and 65 in this series.

[8] Theophany, manifestation of God.

translation of the Bible known as the Septuagint, they slightly modified the text as they translated it from Hebrew into Greek. Where the Hebrew had Yahweh they put "Angel of Yahwe". Compare, for instance, a translation of Exodus (4. 24) made directly from the Hebrew with one based on the Septuagint text. In the latter it is not Yahweh but his Angel who threatens Moses with death. The same applies to Judges (7. 4).

WISDOM

In the oldest accounts wisdom is spoken of as a human quality, the knowledge and skill of the master-craftsman or the artisan (Exod. 28. 1, 3; 35. 30–5; 1 Kings 7. 14). In other places it refers to the king's ability in politics, Solomon is the wise man *par excellence*; he is described as gifted with discernment (3 Kings 3. 9), cunning and generosity (10. 7; 11. 41).

But at a later date, and under the influence of the prophets, "Wisdom" assumes a religious character because it is considered primarily as the distinctive characteristic of Yahweh (Isaias 28. 29; 31. 2). It describes his wonderful design in creating and ruling the earth (Isaias 40. 13; Jer. 10. 12; 51. 15). But it becomes also the prerogative of the Messias for with it God fills his elect (Isaias 11. 2).

In the Sapiential books the word has an even greater force. Job proclaims that God alone knows where wisdom is to be found, because it is his own possession (15. 7–8). Left to himself, man is quite unable to gain it by his own efforts (28. 12, 28).

Proverbs in chapters 8 and 9 presents and describes wisdom. Her dwelling is in God (8. 22) in the sense that she is his gift, he bestows her on those who listen to him (8. 32–4) so that they in their turn may become her dwelling place (8. 2–6 and 35–6). Although she existed before the world (8. 23) her rôle in the great work of creation was only that of spectator of God's wonderful achievements (8. 23–31). But in Chapter 9 she is given a part to play among men, chiefly in the moral order, like that of the counsellor whose wise advice encourages virtue (see as before 8. 32–6).

Ecclesiasticus contains a deeper study of Wisdom which is presented almost as a person. The Lord is her origin (1. 1–10). Her work is to spread abroad over the earth (24), but her special home is in Israel and in Jerusalem (24. 8–11). The beginning of Wisdom is in the fear of the Lord (1. 14) and in his love (1. 10). Meditation on God's own word (1. 5) and on his law (Psalm 118) is also the way to find Wisdom.

The Book of Wisdom describes the spirit of Wisdom as "a good friend to man" and places her side by side with the spirit of the Lord which "fills the whole world" (1. 6, 7) so that together they may teach mankind (9. 17). In chapters 8 (vv. 1 and 6) and 7 (v. 21) she is presented as a conscious and active person, ordering and providing for the world. This is not the case in the Proverbs. In 7. 27, we see that she finds her way into holy men's hearts, turning them into friends and spokesmen of God. In 9. 12, she is named as protector and defender of the righteous among God's people.

To conclude: a thorough study of these texts brings the conviction that to the chosen people Wisdom represented the certainty that Yahweh was present among them. She was not, to their way of thinking, a person to be addressed, but rather God's own activity, of a kind that emphasized the choice he had made of a particular nation. She was a living intermediary, God himself in action. That is the reason why, later on, Christian tradition saw in her a sign of the Word of God, and even identified them. St Luke was to describe Jesus as full of divine Wisdom (2. 40; 4. 22) and his reference was certainly to Isaias 11. 2. But St Paul boldly distinguishes two kinds of wisdom: one purely human, the other which is Christ, the Wisdom of God (1 Cor. 1. 21–30; Col. 1. 15–18).[9] The Epistle to the Hebrews makes the same comparison; it applies the text of Wisdom 7. 26 to the true Son of God who is the "radiance of his Father's splendour" (Heb. 1. 3). In a few cases certain of the Fathers, St Theophilus of Antioch and St Irenaeus for example, have identified Wisdom not with the Word but with the Holy Spirit.

[9] See the explanation of 1 Cor. 21–30 in Chapter III, p. 46.

THE WORD

The Word is closely connected with Wisdom. Three qualities are to be found in it. The Word is creative, being associated with Yahweh in his work of creation: God speaks and all is accomplished (Gen. 1. 3; Ps. 32. 6–9; Isaias 55. 10–11).

The Word is enlightening, given by God to man so that it may make his secrets known (Jer. 1. 9) and in order to guide him and show light on his path (Ps. 118. 105).

The Word both gives judgement on and enacts the divine decrees, and this follows from his creative and enlightening activity. If man would not bow to the word of God, by that Word he would be judged. The most impressive text on this subject is from Wisdom 18. 14–16:

There was a hush of silence all around,
and night had but finished half her swift journey,
when from thy heavenly throne, Lord, down leaped thy word
    omnipotent.

Never lighted sterner warrior on a doomed land;
never was sword so sharp, errand so unmistakable;
thy word that could tread earth yet reach up to heaven.

An evocation such as this suggested itself naturally as a suitable summing up of the work of Christ, King and Judge in glory, in the Apocalypse of St John. The saint sees him riding the earth to bring judgement, with the two-edged sword, symbol of the decree that he must enact, issuing from his mouth (Apoc. 19. 11–15).

Long before the coming of Christ it had been clear that the word of the Messias-King would "strike the earth like a rod" (Isaias 11. 4) and that the rebel nations would be herded "with a crook of iron" (Ps. 2. 9). The Old Testament offered an explanation of the rôle of Christ as judge in glory. Romanesque art of the late tenth century inscribed his impressive personality on the vaults of the crypt of Auxerre cathedral: a Christ of compelling majesty comes to judge the earth, trampling it under the hooves of his white horse. Then the liturgy, in its turn, makes us re-read the wonderful text of the introit of the

Mass for the Sunday within the octave of Christmas in which the Word, whose Incarnation we celebrate at that time, comes as saviour and creator but also as judge. What was prophecy and type has become reality.

THE SPIRIT

To begin with the Spirit of God is action, a manifestation of his rational life and emotions. The inspired authors knew that the Spirit of Yahweh was active (Gen. 1. 2). This spirit he breathed into man, the breath of life that made him like God (Gen. 2. 7). Yet, when he wished, he could take it away (Gen. 6. 3).

To the spirit of God are attributed the mysterious phenomena which are beyond human control: power over the outcome of wars (Judges 3. 10; 6. 34; 11. 29); of carrying men off through the air (3 Kings 18. 12; 4 Kings 2. 9; Acts 8. 39). The Spirit of God inspired the prophets (1 Kings 10. 10; Num. 24. 2; see Acts 2. 4 and 7. 55).

The Spirit of God is said also to dwell in man. By the time of the great prophets the action of the Spirit is no longer seen as intermittent and passing, it has become permanent; the Spirit of the Lord dwells in man to make him act righteously (Isaias 30. 1; see 32. 15; 1 Kings 16. 18). On the other hand, without the Spirit of the Lord the spirit of man goes raving mad (Osee 9. 7).

It is easy to see, then, that it was impossible for the King-Messias to be without it. We see it resting upon him and lavishing its gifts upon him (Isaias 11. 1–6). But also it is understood that when the messianic age comes the hearts of the faithful will be sanctified by it (Joel 3. 1–5). The Acts of the Apostles (2. 16) recounts the fulfilment of this prophecy on the day of Pentecost. Isaias foresaw that perfect peace would distinguish that age (11. 6–9), since the Spirit would dwell in man. Ezechiel prophesied that the Spirit of the Lord would come to breathe new spirit into his people which would change their hearts and make them obedient to the Law of the Lord (36. 23–6). Psalms

50. 12–13 and 103. 29–30 long for or describe this same work of Yahweh in the hearts of men. The liturgy of the fourth Wednesday in Lent, the day on which, in the early Church, after much investigation the names were inscribed of the candidates to receive baptism during the great paschal vigil, is still a baptismal liturgy. It still uses the great passage from Ezechiel, thus recalling to the catechumens and to the Christians of our own age that holy rebirth which the water of baptism effects in their souls. In the following chapter the Spirit of the Lord comes to restore life to the dry bones (37. 1–10). In this way Ezechiel was prophesying the resurrection of Israel, God's people, after the captivity of the exile.

The rôle of the Spirit of the Lord is vividly presented. What is this Spirit in itself? The answer must be: not a distinct person in God but a force, a creative or sanctifying power which comes forth from him to carry out in the world the work which he wishes to accomplish there, particularly when his actions assume a religious character. This idea, moreover, was essential in order to give the Jews a sense of the spiritual and sanctifying activity of Yahweh. It was also—and this applies to the preceding passages as well—a preparation for those souls who would one day be led to think deeply about the particular nature of the Spirit of God, when Jesus should have come to perfect the revelation of that Spirit. That is why the "true Israelites", as St Paul was to call the non-Pharisees, would recognize as a person the Spirit as he is presented in the Acts of the Apostles. Until then it had only been a question of the great deeds accomplished by God, especially in the order of holiness, yet one day they were to learn without surprise that the Holy Spirit had rested on Mary at the Annunciation (Luke 1. 35) and to understand from that fact that the messianic age had come, since the Messias was there, the Spirit resting upon him, just as Isaias had said (7. 14, and 11. 2). Pentecost was to be the pouring out of that same Spirit on the messianic people, as it was written in Joel 3. 1–5 (see Acts 2. 16). To later tradition was to be left the task of describing in detail the particular natures of both Wisdom and the Word of God, as well as that of the Spirit.

THE MANIFESTATIONS OF GOD IN THE OLD TESTAMENT

The name of God is Yahweh, but also "Elohim", which is a plural in Hebrew. What does it mean? Does it conceal a faith in a plurality of Gods? On the other hand, what are we to think of the "theophanies" or manifestations of God which we have already considered? These are two questions to which a short reply must be given.

The plural of the Divine Name

God is called Elohim about two thousand times in the Old Testament. It is admitted that this name, which is in the plural, does not in any way strike at the monotheism of Israel. On the contrary, interpreters of Scripture see in it rather a plural of intensity or of excellence and majesty, meaning that the God of Israel is the only true God. But there is no way in which it can be made to disclose a revelation of the Trinity, however veiled. The Semites lacked the kind of judgement which would have led them to such a development of the idea. For the same reason it cannot be admitted that Genesis 1. 26, in which God-Elohim says: "Let us make man", suggests a joint decision of the three divine Persons. If this plural is attributed to God it is to emphasize the fact that he is a living being and that, above and beyond the importance of the work in hand—that is the creation of man—his liberty is its own cause under the guidance of love. In the same sense God says, after the sin of Adam: "Here is Adam become like one of ourselves" (Gen. 3. 22). God is talking to himself and declares that man, in judging right and wrong, has set himself up as a judge, that is, he is acting like a god.

Similar divine deliberations are to be found in Genesis 11. 7, and in Isaias 6. 8. God is a living God, his thoughts are an assurance of his supreme liberty in all his works.

The Theophanies

The manifestations of God should be interpreted in the same way. From quite early times it was generally believed in

Israel that no one could see God and live (Exod. 33. 20–23, and 3. 6). But other traditions, from a later period, stated on the contrary that Moses and the seventy elders had seen God on the mountain (Exod. 34. 6, 11), and that the people had heard the voice of Yahweh (Deut. 4. 12–15).

More often, however, God did not make a personal appearance in the visions. One of the best known is the vision of Mambre (Gen. 18). Yahweh appeared to Abraham who saw three men standing before him. The Fathers of the Church frequently interpreted this passage as a manifestation of the Trinity. St Ambrose comments: "Abraham saw three men yet he adored in them one God only." This is the sense that the Roman Breviary still gives to the second responsory at Matins for the Thursday after Ash Wednesday. Yet St Hilary said: "Abraham saw three men and adored only one, since he recognized the others as angels." Neither of these interpretations of the scene is quite accurate. In the Old Testament God showed himself and spoke through deputies, a God who was pure spirit could not act otherwise. It followed that when God appeared in human form some other person took his place. This mystery is similar to that of the "Angel of the Lord". God is frequently described as having conversations with those whom he had chosen to carry out particular tasks: with Abraham (Gen. 12. 7; 15. 18; 17. 1); with Isaac (Gen. 26. 2); with Jacob with whom he fought (Gen. 32. 26–31). Already in the earthly Paradise he spoke with Adam and Eve (Gen. 3. 8–24). Another well-known theophany is to be found in Isaias 6. In this case it is the Seraphim, "those who burn with love", who act as a cloak for the divine majesty. Their re-echoing threefold "sanctus" does not proclaim homage to the Trinity but to the infinite holiness of Yahweh.

Another example of theophany is to be found in the idea of the "cloud". The "cloud" or "shekinah" (from a Hebrew verb which means "to dwell") is a sign of the divine presence. Hence the cloud is God's dwelling place. It is usually the sign of his powerful protection as in Exodus 14. 19–20, where Yahweh uses it to protect the retreat of the Hebrews as they flee from Egypt. Behind them it is a dark shade to hide them from the eyes of the Egyptians, before them it shines brightly to light up the night. Under this sign God is both protector and guide. In the tent of assembly the cloud is to be found, showing that God is present there (Exod. 40. 34–5) and again it is seen in the Temple built by Solomon (3 Kings 8. 10–11). We see it overshadowing Mary (Luke 1. 35), showing that God is with her and is working in her. Even in the theophanies it is an intermediary who performs a divine act.

CONCLUSION

Here, then, we have the mystery of God in the Old Testament. The One God is a living God. The living God gives life to men and his envoys cooperate in the work. Thanks to them the spirit of Israel was prepared, or at least had the opportunity to be prepared, to receive a more perfect message, that of the adorable Trinity. But no hint of this mystery was given before the coming of Jesus. It was not until much later that, taught by the New Testament, Christian teachers turned to the Old Testament and applied to God—Father, Son and Holy Spirit—all the riches glimpsed in the texts we have quoted. A fourth-century Father, St Gregory Nazianzen, made the following apposite remarks on the subject of the revelation of the mystery of the Blessed Trinity. They shall form the conclusion of this chapter.

The Old Testament proclaimed the Father quite clearly, and the Son only dimly.[10] The New Testament revealed the Son and allowed us to glimpse the divinity of the Spirit. Now the Spirit dwells among us and shows himself more clearly. When the divinity of the Father[11] was not yet recognized it would not have been prudent openly to proclaim the Son; and when the divinity of the Son was not yet admitted it would not have been fair to impose—I dare to put it like that—a new burden on men by talking to them about the Holy Spirit. Otherwise, like people whose digestions are strained by too rich a diet or who have

[10] Dimly, because like all the Greek Fathers, he held that it was the Son who revealed himself progressively in the theophanies.

[11] That is, of God (monotheism).

stared at the sun's light with eyes still weak from illness, they would have run the risk of losing the strength they had already gained. It was necessary therefore to work towards perfection by stages, by an "upward journey" to use David's phrase (Ps. 83. 6, according to the Greek text); it was necessary to go forward by way of successive clarifications, by increasingly enlightening improvements and advances, in order to see the light of the Trinity shine out at last.[12]

[12] *Fifth Theological Discourse*, No. 26.

CHAPTER II

THE SYNOPTIC GOSPELS OR THE FIRST PREACHING TO JEWS AND GENTILES

THE GRADUAL UNFOLDING OF THE STORY

It was among Jews that Jesus was born. One dogma, mono-theism, was well established in Israel. "There is no Lord but the Lord thy God" (Deut. 6. 4), the pious Israelite repeated. Could God reveal the Trinity to them suddenly, without pre-paration? That would clearly have been useless, for it would have encountered only a refusal to accept it. God, who is a teacher, knows this. Through his Son, whom he sent, he un-veiled the mystery a little at a time. This, then, was Christ's work: to transform this faith in the One God without destroy-ing it, while leaving room for the growth of the idea that in the heart of the strictest monotheism it is necessary to show a plurality of persons living by the same life and equal in all things. It is easy to understand that Jesus, and after Pentecost the apostles, in speaking to the Jews had to follow the law of all human understanding and allow truth to be absorbed gradu-ally. We are well aware of this: when we listen to someone we only acknowledge and feel in his words that degree of truth and power to move us which grows out of our own previous experience, not necessarily out of the possibly much richer experience of the speaker. To a child of six love has only as much meaning as his short experience gives to it. He can scarcely reach beyond plain self-seeking in spite of the concern he seems to feel for his parents and those who care for him. But at twenty-five, when the time comes for engagement and marriage, what profound development has taken place, what altruism is already apparent! And by his fortieth year this same word *love* will carry implications, undertones extending from all that there may have been of imperfection and selfishness in a man's life to the total gift of himself. If, after that, we think of the love of the Curé d'Ars, Teresa or Paul, what fresh revelations each stage of their lives brought to them! How different is this same word *love* when applied to the libertine and to the saint!

The Gospel, then, a book that is divine yet written by men, for men, must also conform to this universal law of revelation. In it the Word of God can be heard in differing degrees of strength, sometimes because God knows the weakness of his hearers and the poverty of their imagination; sometimes because those who receive his revelation cannot understand the indirect ways that he uses in order to reveal himself in a fuller light.

These comments will help us in reading the New Testament. We must be careful not to treat all its books in the same way. It is not that one is holier than another or more truly the word of God, but some of them were written for communities who were already Christian (the writings of St Paul and St John), others for Jewish communities (Matthew and Mark) or for a pagan *milieu* (Luke). Besides, the synoptic accounts were collected together about twenty or thirty years after our Lord's ascension, but before that they had been spoken and formed a body of oral preaching addressed to Jews or Gentiles. With these non-Christian audiences it was often necessary to insinuate the truth rather than state it openly. The apostles, strong in the spirit of Pentecost, were obliged nevertheless to take account of the fact that they were addressing monotheist Jews or pagan Greeks and to reveal to them only gradually the mystery of Jesus and of God. Yet at the same period St Paul was writing to the first Christian communities, as St John was to do still later, without worrying about this gradual teaching. They present the truth in its wholeness and solidity. From this time the words bear a fixed, Christian meaning, and it is no longer the meaning of the Old Testament.

In this spirit we shall read for ourselves some passages from the Synoptists in order to hear their accounts as the Jews heard them. But we shall also read them in the certainty that, in their teaching by word of mouth, the evangelists wanted to impart new truths to the new-born Church. This must be thoroughly understood. The revelation which is given to us in Scripture is founded on the meaning that the author wishes to give to his words and to his story, and not on the meaning which he had at first thought that he found in the words of Jesus. The inspired meaning, written therefore for the Church of all times, is contained in the mind of its author and is revealed for us today in the written word. "It is surely clear to everyone," Pius XII wrote in his Encyclical *Divino Afflante Spiritu*, "that the first rule in interpretation is to find out what the author wanted to say."

It is possible that at first the apostles saw in Jesus only the promised Messias. After Pentecost, we can be quite sure, it is to the Son of God that they bear witness.

TEXTS ON THE TRINITY

The account of the Annunciation

Each verse of the passage in Luke (1. 26–38) is rooted in the Old Testament. 26: The Angel of the Lord brings a message; his name is Gabriel. 27 and 31: He seeks a Virgin called Mary and tells her that she will bear a son to whom she will give the name of Jesus. Now Luke tells us that Mary is a virgin. This is an allusion to the "Almah" of Isaias 7. 14, in which the prophet was foretelling God's decisive intervention for the sake of the coming Messias, prefigured already in the birth of the future king Ezechias, son of Achaz. There the son, who is foreseen as coming in the messianic age, will be called

Emmanuel, that is, "God with us", a prophetic name bearing promise of a divine favour. Here the son of the Virgin Mary is to be called Jesus, a word which in Hebrew means "the Lord saves", and equivalent to "God with us". 28: The angel greets Mary. We usually read "Hail, full of grace", but the Greek word χαῖρε means more than "hail", rather "rejoice", or "break into song" as it is translated in Sophonias 3. 14. Soon it becomes clear why Mary is to rejoice: "the Lord is with her", the angel has told her so; but this certainty rests also on the messianic prophecy as it is given in Zacharias 9. 9: "Glad news for thee, widowed Sion; cry out for happiness, Jerusalem forlorn! See where thy king comes to greet thee."[1]

29–31: Mary is astounded. The angel reassures her: she has found favour with God. It is not difficult to see that this means that her existing state of childlessness (deliberately chosen for the sake of her ideal of virginity)[2] is to end: she is to conceive and bear a son.

32–33: Jesus will be great, he will be called "the son of the most High". This greatness emphasizes God's special care of him, similar to his care of John the Baptist who "will be great in the Lord's eyes" and "filled with the Holy Spirit from his mother's womb" (verse 15). But what follows makes it even clearer. Not only will Jesus be one of the righteous in the sense explained in the previous chapter, he will be *the Messias*: "The Lord God will give him the throne of his father David, he will rule over the house of Jacob for ever and his reign shall never have an end." What the Angel is telling Mary, then, is that the prophecy of Isaias 7. 14, and that in which the prophet Nathan told David that the Messias would be one of his dynasty (2 Kings 7. 12–16), are to be fulfilled in and through her.

35: The son of Mary will also be called "the son of God". But this no longer surprises us, for we know that it was usual

[1] This text took on a new importance when Jesus entered Jerusalem on Palm Sunday, mounted on an ass (Matt. 21. 5).

[2] It was unusual among the Jews to choose to remain a virgin, because childlessness was regarded as a disgrace for a Jewish woman (see Luke 1. 25). But the ideal of virginity was not unknown, as is proved by the documents from Qumran, found near the Dead Sea.

to regard those who were especially privileged by God as his "sons". A great interpreter of Scripture of the fourteenth century, Maldonatus, said that the word of the angel did not indicate what the nature of this "son of God" was to be, but only the manner in which he would come to birth. Because his conception was the result of a divine act, an act of the Holy Spirit, and because the power of the most High had caused a virgin to become fruitful, the child would be holy, "son of God" and "Messias".

There is nothing here with which we are not already familiar. The action of God's Spirit was known to Mary, as was the "cloud", the active presence of the Lord. It seems almost as if there were nothing more in this than in Genesis 18. 14, where the active presence of God rested upon Sarai, so that Isaac should be born to her in spite of her barrenness. The Angel even hints at it in verse 36, quoting the words of the Lord to Mary's ancestress, and addresses them to her in her turn: "Nothing can be impossible with God."

The teaching given in this passage grows clearer. When this scene took place in the obscurity of a humble house in Nazareth it meant, for Mary, that she was to be the mother of the Messias. She could say to herself: It is I who am to bear the Saviour promised to Israel. God said that he was with her, rested upon her in the "cloud" and the "spirit". It was the first indication of the Trinity, still heavily veiled. God was beginning to widen her faith, but Mary was still far from understanding the full depth of the mystery of the Incarnation. She was to let this be seen quite clearly later on, when her Son had reached the age of twelve: "Could you not tell", Jesus said to his parents when they sought him, "that I must needs be in the place which belongs to my Father?" But "these words which he spoke were beyond their understanding" (Luke 2. 49–50).

Yet what is wonderful in this time of preparation is Mary's obedient faith which makes her faithful to God's plan and ready to carry out his will. Her cousin Elizabeth tells her so: "Blessed art thou for thy believing; the message that was brought thee from the Lord shall have fulfilment" (Luke 1. 45).

Mary carries out her part in God's design without the help of any personal revelation, solely through her faith in the Messias-Saviour whose mother she is to be. Her "fiat" expresses her obedience to God, her adoring submission to the one who wishes, through her, to save Israel. Beyond the "fiat" spoken in the present lies the future with its trials, illuminations and all that love can demand.

When Luke wrote down this scene from Mary's own account of it, he knew, because he had received the Spirit of Pentecost which "makes everything plain" (John 14. 26), the significance of the angel Gabriel's message. In recording it he was hinting to Jew and Gentile and revealing to the ages to come, something that was newly discernible in God—the adorable Trinity.

The Baptism of Jesus

Jesus is baptized by John the Baptist.[3] The Holy Spirit comes down upon him in bodily form, like a dove, and a voice is heard from heaven saying: "Thou art *my beloved Son*; in thee I am well pleased."

In order to understand this it is necessary to go back once more to the Old Testament. The voice from heaven is that of the Father. What does he say? The evangelists tell us. The voice quotes Isaias 42. 1, changing two of the terms. Where Isaias put "servant", the evangelists write "Son" and, for "man of my choice", "beloved": "Here is my servant to whom I grant protection, the man of my choice, greatly beloved."

Now in the Greek Septuagint version of the Old Testament the word "beloved" also means "only". For example, in the place where the Hebrew of Genesis 22. 2 and 16 says that Isaac was Abraham's "only" son, the Greek version gives "beloved". The process becomes clear: Greek biblical language uses a word with two meanings: *beloved* and *only*. When the evangelists quote this passage of Isaias 42. 1, they are proclaiming two things: Firstly, that Jesus is the "servant of God" in the biblical sense, the Messias who is spoken of in Isaias 42. 1 and 53, the elect of God who is to bear the weight of the

[3] See Luke 3. 21-2; Matt. 3. 13-17; Mark 1. 9-11.

people's sins. But it also declares that this servant is to be "the son". Secondly, they wish it to be understood that this "servant-son" is "beloved"; that is, chosen above all,[4] hence "only". In other words Jesus is "God's only Son".

The teaching in this passage is now clear. When the by-standers who surrounded Jesus at his baptism heard the heavenly voice, they were being invited to recognize Jesus as the Messias, a Son so privileged that he is even called the "only Son". There was enough in this to make the Israelites think deeply about the meaning of the sonship of Jesus. It is also possible that the bodily form like a dove had already given a hint of the presence of the Spirit of the Lord at work, because this form might well bring to mind the image of Genesis 1. 2: "Over its waters brooded the Spirit of God" (in order to make them fertile). It is unlikely, however, that the Jews saw in this even a glimpse of a manifestation of the Trinity. But when the evangelists assure us that the bodily form like a dove is the Holy Spirit they are instructing us on the use and the nature of his manifestation, as well as on the meaning of this whole theophany. In common with the whole Church we can be sure that in this passage the Gospel is teaching us that Jesus is the Son of the Heavenly Father in the exact sense of the word "Son", and that the third person of the Blessed Trinity rested upon him at his baptism. The pen of the sacred author was inspired in order to give us certainty on this point.

The command to baptize

It is the morning of the ascension, the day that is to bring the separation of Jesus from his own.[5] It is a time for confidences, which means a time for great revelations. Jesus says: "All authority in heaven and on earth has been given to me;

---

[4] We can see the same process at work in the scene of the Trans-figuration (Luke 9. 35). The evangelist uses the same verse of Isaias (42. 1), but he does not use "beloved". The verb used means "chosen above others", hence, unique, and beloved above all.

[5] See Matt. 28. 19.

you, therefore, must go out, making disciples of all nations, and baptizing them in the name of the Father, and of the Son, and of the Holy Ghost."

Christ declares first of all that he had received all authority from the Father. He had already said earlier that the Father had entrusted everything into his hands (Matt. 11. 27). But this is not the only feature by which this last scene is connected with previous revelations. That of the baptism explains it by the parallelism in the two situations. The Father, at the beginning of the public life of his Messias, declared that he possessed all his love and that therefore he should be heard. It was an urgent summons to hear his words and believe them. Now on this last day of his earthly life Christ lifts the last veil from his message. A rite, that of baptism, is to be conferred by the apostles in the name of the three Persons, Father, Son and Holy Spirit. They are persons, for Jesus puts them on a footing of perfect equality in relation to the efficacy of the rite. But it was also a clear declaration that the three are God.

It is with this last revelation that St Matthew closes his Gospel. It was only natural that on that day Jesus should speak out clearly and that later the evangelist should give his readers the last word of the Christian message which is knowledge of the three divine Persons, and especially of the part they play in this rite on which rests the foundation of the Christian religion.

THE PROGRESSIVE REVELATION OF EACH OF THE DIVINE PERSONS

Here again, Father, Son and Holy Spirit are each the object of a revelation which grows into life itself. But it is around the person of Jesus in particular that the new teaching takes shape; and it is through Jesus that the Three-in-One is to be imprinted on the mind and heart of man. Jesus announces his mysterious sonship unobtrusively, and his message is given more fully only as the end of his mission approaches. But it required nothing less than the whole of his earthly life to draw the attention of the Jews to the very special relationship which he claims with God, whom he calls his Father, and with the Holy Spirit. In this way, gradually, the mystery is revealed.

All through his life Jesus strove to bring his disciples to the discovery of his special relationship with God the Father, a relationship utterly transcending their own.

"Could you not tell that I must needs be in the place that belongs to my Father?" (Luke 2. 49). Jesus emphasizes the particular care which he must give to the things that belong to his Father. In other words, he must belong entirely to God, leaving behind him the concerns of Joseph and Mary. But his words were beyond their understanding (verse 50).

Jesus claims to be "the Son of God" on other grounds than those on which men may claim this title. On this subject read Matt. 6. 32; 7. 21; 10. 32; 12. 50; Luke 11. 13; 12. 32.

He is called "Son of God" by Satan (Matt. 4. 1–11), by the devils (Matt. 8. 20) and by the centurion when he is dying on the cross (Matt. 27. 54). But it will be noticed that nothing in these passages makes it possible to say what kind of sonship unites Jesus with his Father. It is even necessary to reject the idea that he was believed to be the Son of God in the sense of equal with God. Did not the crowd say, "Is not this the carpenter, the son of Mary?" (Mark 6. 3). And sometimes he is called "Son of David" meaning the Messias (Matt. 9. 2; 12. 23; 20. 30–4; 21. 9).

Whenever the Messias performs miracles people are surprised that he should be able to do so. To make them ask questions, to encourage reflection about himself, to be a sign which men refuse to acknowledge, as Simeon had foretold (Luke 2. 34), is what Jesus wants. There was some mystery about him.

There is a beautiful text of great significance spoken by Jesus in Matthew 11. 25–7. In it he states that none knows the Father truly except the Son, and that he himself has a superior knowledge of the Father, a knowledge which is his to communicate to whom he pleases.

This declaration has enormous force. It can only be interpreted as referring to knowledge in the most complete sense, which alone makes possible an unequalled intimacy between

Father and Son. The Old Testament was certainly well aware that God alone knows his own plans (Isaias 40. 13). If, then, Jesus knows them too, it is because he is God. In this lies the great importance of this declaration. We cannot help asking what echo his words can have found in the hearts of his disciples. What happened afterwards shows clearly enough that they did not understand immediately. In fact, not long afterwards Jesus and the twelve are at Caesarea Philippi and Jesus is trying to find out what they believe about him (Matt. 16. 13–21). We must read this passage carefully. Peter's profession of faith still implies only a recognition of Jesus as Messias. It is true that St Matthew reports Peter as saying "Thou art the Christ, the Son of the living God", but Mark gives only "Thou art the Christ" (8. 29) and St Luke "The Christ whom God has anointed" (9. 20). And that, at the time, was what Jesus wanted people to say about him. He knew that they were asking themselves all sorts of questions, but no clear statement had as yet been made about him. People said, "He is the carpenter's son", or "He is the son of Mary and Joseph". There was some doubt about him, and for many he was a stone of stumbling. The story of the calming of the storm suggests a number of very helpful ideas (Mark 4. 35–41). It shows Jesus giving proof of extraordinary powers, powers that invite comparison with those that the Lord showed in the story recorded in Jonas 1. 3–15. There it was Jonas who slept in the ship, unworried by the storm. That storm was calmed only when the sailors had prayed to the Lord and Jonas had been thrown into the sea. Here, the storm is stilled when, once roused from sleep, Jesus commands it. The two situations are remarkably alike, with the exception that it is no longer the Lord who calms the waves but Jesus himself. It was this that immediately threw everyone into a state of fear, but a holy fear, a fear that is felt as a clear manifestation of divine power. Jesus was a mystery to all of them. No one yet dared to assert that he was sent from God, but they asked themselves: "Who is this who is obeyed even by the winds and the sea?"

It was Peter, then, the leader whom Jesus was to put at the head of the others, for whom was reserved the honour and

grace of speaking the crucial word. Peter proclaims his faith in
the Christ of God. For the time being that was enough because
it was necessary for the community of Israel to recognize its
Messias. And this is again asserted by Peter on the day of
Pentecost: "God has made him Master and Christ, this Jesus
whom you crucified" (Acts 2. 36). So, when Peter had spoken
in the name of them all, a step forward had been taken: it had
been proclaimed that the Christ was there in the midst of his
people, that the Messianic age had come. For the twelve, it
meant the knowledge that God's salvation had come to them;
all the same, it was not yet time for it to be poured out upon
all. For this reason Jesus forbade his disciples to tell anyone
that he was the Christ (Matt. 16. 20).

How weak and wavering was Peter's faith! A few moments
later the privileged apostle was to show quite clearly that he
had not yet grasped the depths of the mystery or all the
characteristics of the Messias. If he had, would he have rejected
in such a way the idea that the Christ of God must suffer?
(Matt. 16. 22). What a difference between this moment when,
on a point of such importance, Peter shows ignorance and lack
of courage in his faith, and that other moment when he was
to speak with emotion of the spotless Lamb who had redeemed
him, as Isaias had prophesied (Isaias 53; 1 Peter 1. 18–21). At
this period of his spiritual maturity there was no longer anything shocking to him in the idea of the suffering servant.
Through the discovery—the work of the Spirit (John 14. 26)—
of the divinity of Jesus, in the light of Easter morning and
the tongues of fire of Pentecost, Isaias 53 had been transfigured
for him.

In the parable of the unfaithful vine-dressers (Matt.
21. 33–46) Jesus relates how they put to death first the servants,
then *the Son*. This contrast between the Son, the heir to the
vineyard, and the servants who are simply charged with the
care of the harvest emphasizes the preeminence of Jesus: he
surpasses the prophets who preceded him. This is a transcendence which none of the Jews could fail to understand: from
that moment they began to desire his death.

A little later Jesus compels the Pharisees to acknowledge

that he whom they know to be the *son* of David is also his *Master*:

> The Lord said to my Master,
> sit on my right hand.

This means: "The Lord (Yahweh) said to my Master (the Messias who will be descended from me, David) 'Sit on my right hand.'" "If, then", Jesus concludes, "David calls Christ his Master, how can he be also his son?" (Matt. 22. 41–6). We must also bear in mind the text of Matthew 26. 63–6. To Caiphas who is questioning him Jesus declares that he is "the Son of God". This statement is regarded as a blasphemy. Why?

It will be noticed that Jesus, at this solemn moment when his life is at stake, asserts first of all that he is the Messias spoken of in Daniel 7. 13: He "is seated at the right hand of God's power and comes on the clouds of heaven". But the characteristics of the Messias in this passage of Daniel are heavenly ones because of his mysterious origin: he will come "on the clouds of heaven". On the other hand Jesus' origins are known to all to be earthly: he is the son of Joseph and Mary. Hence, in the eyes of Caiphas, the incredible nature of Jesus' words: how can he be the Messias-Son of God of whom Daniel speaks? His pretension passes all bounds and issues in blasphemy. Here again the exact nature of the sonship of Jesus is almost certainly not even glimpsed, but who can doubt that Matthew, the inspired writer, wishes to teach us the divine origin and nature of God's envoy?

St Matthew tells us that wonders followed the death of Jesus on the cross: earthquakes, rocks splitting open, rising of the dead, and so on. The centurion and his men in charge of the crucifixions were seized with terror and cried out: "No doubt but this man was the son of God" (27. 54). What did this exclamation mean? Consider the context of the scene. This worthy Roman soldier was utterly ignorant of what a true "son of God" might be. But his attention had been drawn to Christ a little while before by a suggestion made about him ("Let us see whether Elias is to come and save him"), and now he cannot help expressing his conviction that Jesus is truly a just man. That, in fact, is the exclamation that St Luke attributes to him, and which, if it does not bear the mark of greater truth, at least explains his meaning better: "This was indeed a just man" (Luke 23. 47).

In the story of the meeting of Jesus and the two disciples at Emmaus (Luke 24. 26–47) the risen Christ still states nothing more than the glorification of the suffering Messias of Isaias 53: "Then he enlightened their minds to understand the scriptures; So it was written, he told them, and so it was fitting that Christ should suffer, and should rise from the dead on the third day."

The Spirit of God has taken possession of the souls of the apostles. The Spirit, we can be sure, has shown them the truth, as Jesus had said (John 15. 26). All the same, the apostles, faithful to Jesus' own method, were to develop their teaching in the same gradual way, with the same prudence. Or, to put it better, the slow but spiritually stimulating method that they use is the one which is to be found in the synoptic Gospels.

In the Acts of the Apostles they can be seen taking as their starting point the "Servant" of the Lord (Isaias 42. 1, and 53) in order to declare that Jesus is, not the "Son of God", but his "servant" (3. 13). God is still the God of Abraham, Isaac and Jacob, but he is also the God who has "brought honour to his son Jesus" whom the Jews had given up and disowned before Pilate. But from being the servant (3. 13–26; 4. 27, 30, etc.) he has become, through his resurrection, Master and Christ—the one, in fact, whose coming as Saviour was awaited (2.32–6).[6] But when he was on earth, Jesus, according to St Luke, was only a man "accredited" by God in the miracles which he worked (Acts 2. 22). The voice of St Paul will be needed to give to the expression "Son of God" a more than purely messianic meaning.

We can only conclude that the early preaching of the apostles, or at least as much of it as was recorded in the Acts and in the synoptic Gospels in the middle of the first century, stated that Jesus was the *Christ of God*, the *Son of his choice*, the *only* Son, beloved above all. We must certainly not see in

---

[6] We shall discover more of the significance of the title "Lord" in St Paul's writings, in the next chapter.

this a lack, even after Pentecost, in the apostles' own knowledge of Jesus; it is rather a desire to present their Master in such a way that their hearers could accept him without scandal. They themselves knew quite well that the Master had acted in this way with them and with all the others, otherwise he would have been stoned on the spot. Did not the law of Moses forbid that they should recognize as God any other than the Lord? (Exod. 10. 5; Deut. 6. 5). But Jesus, and the apostles after him, built on these foundations. They forced men to recognize his presence, to reflect on his words and examine his deeds closely, so that they might discover in them the mystery of his relationship to the Father and the mystery of his own person. One example will serve as a summary of his method. The Lord, and he alone, had the right to demand the absolute devotion of every creature. He presented himself as the sole object of love: "Listen then, Israel; there is no Lord but the Lord thy God, and thou shalt love the Lord thy God with the love of thy whole heart, and thy whole soul, and thy whole strength" (Deut. 6. 4–5).

Jesus in his turn demands that same love which, admitting no rival, demands a willingness even to leave all to follow him. But in thus making himself the centre of man's religion Christ was to some extent usurping the Lord's prerogatives, he was indeed a sign to be contradicted. He firmly upheld the principle of Deuteronomy (Matt. 22. 37). He also maintained that men must follow him and that he had the right to reward those who were faithful to him (Matt. 10. 38; 19. 27–9; Luke 9. 23; 22. 28–30). This claim was stronger than all the rest and the dualism of these diverse declarations could only be resolved by one single affirmation: Jesus is God as the Lord is God, and forms with him only one God. But considerable mental agility was necessary to resolve these contradictions, to assert at the same time that the Lord is alone to be served (Matt. 4. 10) and that Jesus is not an impostor because the Father has declared him to be his "beloved son" (Matt. 3. 17; 17. 5), and to follow this up to the fullest extent and admit that Jesus is what he seems to be claiming to be. It is in the light of this that the passage in Matthew (11. 25–7) ought to have been understood from the beginning. But Jesus was declaring precisely that it was only through humility that any one could receive his revelation: "Father, who art Lord of Heaven and earth, I give thee praise that thou hast hidden all this from the wise and the prudent and revealed it to little children!"

Before being known as the Son of God, Jesus must first of all be thought of as a fact. It was necessary that he should be examined as such, simply, without preconceived ideas. It must be recognized that the fierce monotheism of a people who lived by the Law alone, to whom it was the rock that supported them, would put serious obstacles in the way of such a process. The arrogance of the Pharisees had made of the Law a visor that only humility could raise. Until that was done spiritual blindness would remain the Jews' affliction.

St Gregory Nazianzen was far-seeing when he assured us that the era that began at Pentecost was the era of the Holy Spirit, whose manifestation is made clear in the Church. It is not surprising then if, here again, in the synoptic Gospels and in the Acts, the revelation of the Spirit takes place as a prolongation of the Old Testament, if he is first seen as a power coming from God rather than a divine Person. It was for the Church to discern his personal nature.

The angel Gabriel had said that John the Baptist would be filled with the Holy Spirit from his mother's womb (Luke 1. 15). It was the sign of his prophetic vocation, analogous to that of Jeremias (1. 5) and to that of the Messias (Isaias 11. 1–5). In the same sense Matthew (1. 18–20) and Luke (1. 35) attribute the virgin birth of Jesus to the work of the Holy Spirit.

But in order the better to accredit his mission the Holy Spirit is with Jesus and guides him throughout the course of his life: he is with him at his baptism (Luke 3. 22); he sends him into the desert (Luke 4. 1); he leads him into Galilee (Luke 4. 14); by his action Jesus is filled with gladness (Luke 10. 21); Jesus casts out devils by his power (Matthew 12. 28); but in his turn he promises to bestow the Spirit on the apostles, either in a quite general way (Luke 24. 49; Acts 1. 5 and 8) or else to help them in particular ways. For instance, they will be inspired with the right words when they are falsely accused (Mark 13. 11). The Spirit of the Lord, then, becomes the Spirit of Jesus; it is his possession, above all he can use it as he wishes.

The Acts of the Apostles, a book which is wonderful because of the rôle the Holy Spirit plays in it, might more suitably be called the Acts of the Holy Spirit. It is filled with his presence. Jesus has kept his word; the Spirit has come, the gift of the Master now in glory (2. 33). His name is "Spirit", or "Holy Spirit", or "Spirit of the Lord" (5. 9; 8. 39) and once "the Spirit of Jesus" (16. 7). The coming of the Spirit is bound up with certain rites: with baptism (1. 5; 2. 38; 11. 15), the laying on of hands (8. 15–19; 19. 6); he comes upon those who listen to the apostles' words (2. 4; 10. 44).

The effects he produces on the faithful are extraordinary but sometimes only temporary, for the purposes of a particular function or mission: the gift of speaking strange languages (2. 4, 11; 10. 46), of prophecy (11. 28; 20. 22, 23), of wisdom (6. 10), of courage in bearing witness (4. 8, 31). But we are also told that he makes his dwelling in them permanently (6. 3; 11. 24), which is not surprising if we remember that this was already one of his prerogatives in the Old Testament.

This Holy Spirit was the Spirit that dwelt in Jesus during his lifetime (1. 2; 10. 38). According to the Gospels he had guided Jesus; now he guides the apostles: he orders Philip the deacon to go and preach to the Ethiopian (8. 29); for Peter he indicates the line he should take in his relations with the Gentile, Cornelius (10. 19 and 11. 12); he chooses Barnabas and Saul as missionaries (13. 2–4); he prevents their going to Asia in order to send them to Troas (16. 6–8).

We know also that it was he who inspired the Scriptures; who else, then, should make their meaning clear? (1. 16; 2. 16; 4. 25; 7. 51). Through him the meaning of the Old Testament is made clear, and just as he had inspired its authors so also he guides the apostles in governing the Church and preserves them from error. At the first Council held at Jerusalem it is he who dictates the decisions to be taken (15. 28). A power at work, a light, a guide to the leaders of the Church: such is the Spirit in the Acts.

But there is more than this. The Holy Spirit is treated as a person, especially in the way in which a parallel is drawn between him and Jesus. In the same way that Jesus sends Ananias to Saul to tell him what to do (9. 10) the Holy Spirit sends Peter to Cornelius (10. 19). In the same way that Jesus would not allow Paul to stay in Jerusalem but sent him among the Gentiles (9. 15), so, in his turn, the Holy Spirit was later to prevent his journey into Bithynia in order to send him to Troas (16. 7). Finally, the Spirit is again spoken of as a person when Peter reproaches Ananias with having defrauded the Holy Spirit (5. 3 and 9). Jesus himself had declared that blasphemy against the Holy Spirit would not be forgiven (Matt. 12. 31).

The Church has been careful to preserve this teaching. She knows that the guide who led her through her first campaigns in a world still hostile and closed to Christ, remains always her light and her defender. Every year at Pentecost she repeats the words of the wonderful sequence:

O lux beatissima,   Light immortal, Light divine,
Reple cordis intima   Visit thou these hearts of thine,
Tuorum fidelium.   And our inmost being fill.

CHAPTER III

THE MESSAGE OF ST PAUL

THE SPIRIT OF ST PAUL

St Paul's message differs from that of the synoptic Gospels for several reasons. First of all, Paul is a convert. We know how he was halted by the glorified Christ on his way to Damascus to persecute the Christians. Christ had "won the mastery over him" as he was to say later (Philipp. 3. 12); it was a sudden overwhelming conversion. So it was he "to whom all glory belongs" whom he first encountered (1 Cor. 2. 8), and he it is who always holds the first place in his heart, the Christ delivered up by the Jews, but triumphant over death by the power of God the Father who raised him up (Philipp. 2. 9–11). In the foreground of St Paul's work we must always see this Christ, dead for our sins and raised up so that we may rise also (1 Cor. 15. 3–4 and 8–9). We can see, then, that Paul's spiritual journey was quite different from that of the other apostles. They came gradually to a knowledge of their Lord. They knew first "the man Jesus", the son of Joseph and Mary. They heard his summons to leave their work as fishermen (Matt. 4. 18–22), or tax-collector (Matt. 9. 9). It is hardly surprising that they took such pleasure in recounting his life in the flesh. Almost in contradiction St Paul's attention is concentrated on Christ's death and glorious resurrection, the major actions of his life. It is only by allusion that he refers to the earthly Christ (for instance, Rom. 1. 1–5; Gal. 4. 4, etc.).

What also gives a special character to St Paul's message is his profound and immediate knowledge of Christ. If we went by certain of his sayings we should be tempted to think that no teacher intervened between Christ and himself: "The gospel I preached to you is not a thing of man's dictation; it was not from man that I inherited or learned it, it came to me by a revelation from Jesus Christ" (Gal. 1. 11–12). But these verses were written impulsively, to vindicate his right to the title of apostle which had been contested (Gal. 1. 1). His faithful disciple St Luke took care to let us know that it was not Jesus' wish to be Paul's immediate director. After his conversion it was to Ananias that he sent him, and it was from him that he received all the instruction he needed in order to carry out his mission as an apostle (Acts 9. 6, and 11–17). For in the Church even St Paul must be taught by her leaders. At that time the mission of preaching the Gospel belonged to the Twelve and from them Paul received the essential message of Christ: he admits this to the Corinthians (1 Cor. 11. 23). But what left such a deep mark on him was not so much that he had been instructed by this man or that but that he had been specially chosen by Jesus as the apostle of the heathen (Gal. 1. 1 and 16). It was impossible for this choice not to give a special quality of warmth to his message. In one moment the persecutor had turned into an apostle: such an experience inevitably marked Paul's soul for ever. The fiercely monotheist Jew, ferreting out the disciples of Christ, knew from that moment that the one God, whom indeed he did not renounce (Col. 3. 20), had nevertheless a Son through whom he accomplished the redemption of the world (Rom. 3. 23–5; Col. 1. 12–14). The Law in which the Pharisee gloried (Rom. 3. 21) gave place to the grace of Christ.

Finally, the message of St Paul was thought out and written for a *milieu* very different from that to which the synoptic Gospels were addressed. Their purpose was to show the Jews that Jesus was the Messias, and the Son of God in a unique manner. Paul sent his letters of direction to Christian churches. His correspondents had already been given their first instruction in the faith. It was no longer necessary to teach them their ABC but to strengthen them, to reveal to them the full breadth of God's eternal plan for mankind, to invite them to enter more deeply into the intimate life of the divine Persons. We must not be surprised that Paul felt no need to prove to them that Christ is God. It is a weakness of our present-day faith to demand apologetic arguments so that we can propound them to those who should no longer need them. Paul preferred to describe the mystery of Father, Son, and Holy Spirit. The rudiments of the faith, which are suitable for the state of spiritual childhood (1 Cor. 13. 11), must give way to more adult fare. His correspondents asked of him teaching which should set forth for them all that the Christian life might demand. St Paul could not refuse them. It is to this that we owe the ardent words in which he shows us the Blessed Trinity ever at work for our salvation.

THE DIVINE PERSONS

Saul had learned that the one God consisted of Father, Son and Holy Spirit. Henceforward, in Paul's view, the whole of Christian life was governed by this revelation. For Father, Son and Spirit are not simply three Persons living in some unimaginable realm forbidden to men. In making themselves known through the Son all three give themselves also in him. Each one looks upon us with goodwill. Each works in his own way, principally for our sanctification. At the same time they remain always closely united: one does nothing without another, nothing outside another. It is the certainty of this that allows us to draw the conclusion of their identity of nature.

THE FATHER

Who and what is he?

It is not unimportant to notice that in St Paul's use of language the Father is called "God", with the exception of Romans 9. 5, Philipp. 2. 6 and Titus 2. 14, where this name is applied to Christ. In the Old Testament "God" meant the Lord, the one God. St Paul reserves it for the One of whom it is said that he is "God, the Father of our Lord Jesus Christ" (Rom. 15. 6; see also 2 Cor. 1. 3; 11. 31; Ephes. 1. 3). "God" is truly the name that belongs to the Father since we are told that he sent his Son into the world (Rom. 8. 3 and 32). But he is presented to us, by this very fact, as the *source* of love: the most precious thing is his to give. Love comes from God the Father (2 Cor. 13. 13); it is his prerogative, we might say his attribute, and it is by the Holy Spirit that he sends it (Rom. 5. 5). St John puts it still better: the Father who sends his Son (John 3. 16; 1 John 4. 10) is *Love* (1 John 4. 8).

The Father, the beginning of our salvation

Everyone knows that Christ does not condemn sinners since he came to save them (Matt. 9. 13; Luke 19. 10). Are we equally certain that the Father is not the God of vengeance that certain writers used to take pleasure in presenting to us? If there are souls still enslaved by servile fear, let them open the writings of St Paul. The Apostle reassures us. God the Father, who is the Source of love, was the Saviour of men before Jesus was. It is to him first of all that we owe our redemption.

The Law of Moses—the converted Pharisee knows it—was powerless to save mankind (Rom. 3. 28). So the Father intervened: "There was something the law could not do, because flesh and blood could not lend it the power; and this God has done by sending us his own Son, in the fashion of our guilty nature, to make amends for our guilt. He signed the death warrant of sin in our nature" (Rom. 8. 3). This manifestation of the Father's love restored peace to the soul of Paul: "But here, as if God meant to prove how well he loved us, it was while we were still sinners that Christ, in his own appointed time, died for us. All the more surely then, now that we have found justification through his blood, shall we be saved through him from God's displeasure" (Rom. 5. 8–9). Faced with such certainty Pascal cried out: "Joy, joy, joy, tears of joy!"

It is to the Father that we owe our salvation. But what is the vocation of the redeemed? St Paul tells us in a few words, the most impressive in his theology. Here again it is to the Father that we must look for the explanation. "We are well aware that everything helps to secure the good of those who

love God, those whom he has called in fulfilment of his design."
It is in this calling that we must seek for the meaning of our
vocation. For it is nothing else than to be "destined from the
first to be moulded into the image of his Son, who is thus to
become the eldest-born among many brethren" (Rom. 8. 28–9;
see also Ephes. 1. 4–5 and 11). The Son, then, is "the true
likeness of the God we cannot see" (Col. 1. 15), that is, an
exact reproduction of him, it is tempting to say "his photo-
graphic copy". This he is for all eternity. As for us, it is in
earthly time that we are called to be the image of the image,
to reproduce him. So the Son is to become the eldest-born
among many brethren, "called" in him to this extraordinary
vocation, "justified" and already glorified in his glorification
(Rom. 4. 25). What confidence and what boldness must follow
from this, since we become "sons of God" and so may call
God "Father" (Rom. 8. 15–16).

Already the origin of the salvation granted to us in his Son,
the Father is also its provider in this age which is that of the
Church. His Spirit brings it to us by pouring his love into
our hearts (Rom. 5. 5).

The Father, the end for which Redemption is planned

Too often our thoughts slip into a view of redemption centred
on man. Since Renaissance humanism placed him at the centre
of the universe, he has become the sole explanation of the
sending of the Son among us; practically speaking the ransoming of man is for us the only key to the work of redemption.
From this follows the narrowness of our view of the world.
"We must save it," we say, "we must bring God to it." It is
true that this is a very real aspect of things, certainly it was for
us that the Son was born, died and rose again. But it is not
enough to say that. In the mind of St Paul the Redemption is
not so much the saving of man by bringing God to him, as the
returning of man to God to whom he belongs. The Father's
purpose in sending the Son to save the world is, through the
Son, to reconcile it with himself.

There are few passages more illuminating than Colossians 1. 20: "It was God's (the Father's) good pleasure to let all completeness dwell in him (Christ) and through him to win back all things, whether on earth or in heaven, into union with himself, making peace with them through his blood shed on the cross." And it is a reconciliation bringing peace: "This (becoming a new creature in Christ) as always is God's doing; it is he who through Christ, has reconciled us to himself, and allowed us to minister this reconciliation of his to others. Yes, God was in Christ, reconciling the world to himself, establishing in our hearts his message of reconciliation instead of holding men to account for their sins" (2 Cor. 5. 18–19).

We can go further. Paul sets before us an impressive vision of the end of the world's history (1 Cor. 15. 24–8). On this earth the Son will destroy all evil power, making it subject to himself who has received all power for that purpose (Ps. 2. 2). God the Father himself has placed the whole universe under his feet (Ps. 7. 7). But the end must come. In that day the Father will say, "now all is made subject, save Christ". Then the Son will return to him his kingdom and will himself be subject to the Father who has made all things subject to him. And God the Father shall be all in all.

The climax of world history is perhaps not so much the cross and resurrection of Jesus as this last day when all things will be made subject to the Father. The words of Ignatius, the aged Bishop of Antioch, on his way to martyrdom become understandable: at the very moment that he seemed to be conquered by the "powers of this world" hating Christ in his person, his desire was to imitate Christ, it was Christ he sought, Christ that he wanted (*Epistle to the Romans* 7. 1). To be ground by the teeth of wild beasts would make of him an "image of the Son". Yet he knew that this was not the limit to his soul's longing. The Spirit was there to murmur in his heart "come to the Father" (7. 2).

The Father as the final purpose of redemption—that is an idea that might change a whole life. What we are aiming at is no longer "I", or "my salvation", it is to exult and rejoice in the Church before him who has willed our salvation. And, yet higher still, it is the vocation of the redeemed to make hymns of adoration and praise re-echo before the majesty of the eternal Father, hymns which we rehearse even now in the Preface of our Mass: *nos tibi (Pater), semper et ubique gratias agere*.

THE SON

What is the meaning for Paul of the Christ whom he met on the road to Damascus? What must he mean to the Christian communities in his charge? By the various names that he gives to him, St Paul tells us.

The title of "Son"

St Paul uses the name readily. He says "Son" without an epithet (Rom. 1. 3 and 9; 5. 10; 8. 29; 1 Cor. 1. 9; 15. 28; Gal. 1. 16; 1 Thess. 1. 10). "The Son of God" in the fullest sense (Rom. 1. 4; 2 Cor. 1. 19; Gal. 2. 20). "God's *own* Son", that is, his only Son, whom he delivers up for us in imitation of Abraham who did not spare his "only son"[1] (Gen. 22. 2 and 16; Rom. 8. 3 and 32). He is also the "beloved Son" (Col. 1. 13), the adjective "beloved" being, as we know, the equivalent of "only" and of "own".

We can see again in this passage the idea already emphasized above: it is God the Father who delivers us from the "power of darkness", that is, from the power of the devil, in order to give us a place in the kingdom of his beloved Son. The prophecy of Psalm 2. 8 finds its fulfilment here: "Thou shalt have the nations for thy patrimony; the very ends of the world for thy domain."

Christ, the Wisdom of God

St Paul does not use this name very often. We only meet it twice, and in the same passage (1 Cor. 1. 24 and 30). In spite of its rarity, the Apostle puts such a richness of meaning into the expression that it sums up one whole aspect of his theology. What does he mean when he calls Christ the "wisdom of God"

[1] See previous chapter.

—that is, the wisdom of the Father? The expression needs to be seen in its place in the main current of his thought and clarified by referring to the Old Testament. The difficulty, at Corinth, was to proclaim that Jesus crucified was God. Faced by Greek civilization, the Corinthians felt themselves at a disadvantage. Avid for "wisdom", that is, for philosophy, the Greeks elaborated magnificent logical systems that placed them among the great thinkers of the human race. We owe to the "Greek miracle" the highest conceptions of both divine and earthly realities.

But if Greek "wisdom" gave a satisfactory explanation of man it refused to make room for the intervention of an almighty divine power. For the Greek the world was not created but eternal and without history; or, better still, it was perpetually beginning again and quite beyond the reach of interference by any superior being. Time is cyclic and repeats itself indefinitely. We cannot find a better comparison with the Greek world than our own materialist and determinist century, which uses such ideas to escape the control that might be imposed by a God whose very name has become meaningless. The Greek world, like that of the scientists, was self-sufficient. But to understand the universe, to provide a philosophical explanation of man who inhabits it, there was the "wisdom" on whose possession the Greeks prided themselves. To talk to them about an incarnate God or, worse still, one crucified for us, only made them shout with laughter. Paul heard them at Athens, on the Areopagus, when, after a beautiful speech that sacrificed more than a little to human wisdom, he had introduced the note of Christian hope, the resurrection of the dead in Christ. They made fun of him (Acts 17. 22–32). After this almost total defeat Paul left for Corinth, but the lesson did him good, and on arrival there it was another kind of wisdom that he proclaimed (1 Cor. 2. 1–5), not that of the learned philosophers but the wisdom that comes from God.

The wisdom which he wanted to preach from then on was first of all the manifestation of a divine attribute: that wisdom which is the great plan of God as provider, steersman, ruler of the world. As he tells the Romans, the wisdom of God is so apparent in his works that it was inexcusable of the heathen not to have recognized it, and through it the Creator (Rom. 1. 19–20). One of the wise men of the Old Testament had already said that God's power, through his wisdom, swept from world's end to world's end, graciously ordering all things (Wisdom 8. 1). Wisdom is a kind of signature that God puts on all his work, inviting men to bow before his creative and providential intervention.

The beauty of creatures cannot but draw man upwards to the incomparable beauty of the Creator (Wisdom 13. 3–5). All this was still very Greek in its method. Plato said nearly the same thing in his *Banquet*. The Wise Man, and St Paul after him, only added the idea of a Divine providence. But this was insufficient to distinguish the Christian from the Greek: Christianity owes its originality to the fact that the Son of God entered this world. This was the gulf to be crossed, one which would divide the two wisdoms for ever. Paul did not hesitate. The Christian God took part in the ordering of the world even to the extent of recreating it by his death. It was no longer a question of human wisdom; God himself had made plain the darkest labyrinths of history in his Son, "the Wisdom of God". It was a bold stroke to compare "the wisdom of the wise men" of this world with the "wisdom of God" made manifest in the weakness of man. This idea of a God incarnate and, worse, crucified (1 Cor. 1. 23), was to the Gentiles mere folly, to the Jews a stumbling block. But "so much wiser than men is God's foolishness; so much stronger than men is God's weakness" (25). The weakness and ignominy of the cross is nevertheless "God's wisdom". Here is the key to the interpretation of the world and of the drama of man: sin and grace can only be explained in Christ crucified, "the wisdom of God".

Does this mean that, in itself, the cross of Christ is enough to explain the redemption of sin; that it is itself "the wisdom of God"? This is not strictly true. If the "wisdom of God" reveals its splendour through the crucified Christ it is because he is primarily the perfect expression of the substance of the Father. The prologue to the Epistle to the Hebrews, which is rich in St Paul's theology, applies a text of scripture boldly.

The book of Wisdom (7. 26) proclaimed that the Wisdom which comes forth from God is "the glow that radiates from eternal light . . . the untarnished mirror of God's majesty . . . the faithful echo of his goodness".

But the wisdom of the Old Testament, whose only function was to show forth the loving kindness of God's power, becomes, in the Epistle, Christ himself. Here he is called "radiance of the Father's splendour, and the full expression of his being" (1. 3). In other words Christ radiates God, reveals him, shows him, because he is his exact reproduction. The seal leaves in the wax an imprint identical with the design it bears. It is a faithful image of it. Christ, "God's image", whose features shine with his glory (2 Cor. 4. 4–6), is God himself. By calling Christ "God's wisdom", St Paul was giving the Corinthians an incomparable instruction on his divinity and on the scope of his work in this world. At one stroke he compared two civilizations, two ways of salvation—human wisdom and "God's wisdom"—declaring that the only true and saving one was that which seemed weak and feeble to the wise in this world's fashion, so that "no creature was to have any ground for boasting, in the presence of God. It is from him that you take your origin, through Christ Jesus, whom God gave us to be all our wisdom, our justification, our sanctification and our atonement; so that the scripture might be fulfilled, If anyone boasts, let him make his boast in the Lord" (1 Cor. 1. 29–31).

Christ the Lord

This is the third title which must be considered. However important the expressions "Son" and "Wisdom" may be, they cannot compare with the glorious title which according to St Paul is the name proper to Christ.

What is the reason for this? It springs from St Paul's basic idea that Jesus Christ possesses an all-powerful and universal Lordship, the same that the Old Testament attributes to Yahweh and that no true Jew would have dared to deny him. The word "Lord", a translation of the Hebrew *Adonai*, of the Greek κυρίος, and of the Latin *Dominus*, all words which evoke the idea of the *universal Lordship* that belongs to

Yahweh, has a whole history to itself which it is useful to understand in order to grasp St Paul's thought, and perhaps also to understand the persecution which was one of the first tragedies of early Christianity.

The word Lord was used in two ways, in both Jewish and other non-Christian civilizations.

It had a secular use. "Lord" in that case was usually a form of courtesy, rather like the title of "Monsignor" for Church dignitaries. Abraham used it in this way when he spoke to Yahweh by the oaks of Mambre (Gen. 18. 3, 27, 30–2), the Canaanite woman used it to Jesus in Phoenicia (Mark 7. 28). Such a title, from the lips of this woman, emphasized the purely human reverence which she felt in his presence. Mary Magdalen showed the same feeling when she spoke to the man she took for a gardener on the morning of the resurrection (John 20. 15). In Rome, "Lord" emphasized the power of the Emperor over his subjects, power like that of a master over his slaves: the "Lord" is the "despot". The soldier-emperors, like Augustus, included in the title the right which they claimed to mobilize their subjects for war. Augustus was invested with this title of "Lord" as a sign of his sovereign power over his Empire. In the Acts of the Apostles (25. 26) Festus says to Agrippa: "writing to my sovereign Lord, I have no clear account to give . . ." writing, that is, to the Emperor, who was master in these affairs.

The Greeks, who had no liking for the feel of a dictator's rod, did not use the title of "Lord" either for Philip of Macedonia or for Alexander, military geniuses though they both were. "Lord" meant a man who was the legal owner of property.

But after a while things changed. Under Nero and Domitian, perhaps already under Caligula, the title of "Lord" took on a new meaning. To command armies, to be "Lord" of an Empire, was no longer enough for these new despots. As of old in Egypt, they made themselves "gods" and claimed divine honours. So it happened that, like Daniel who had once refused to pray to King Darius when he ordered it because he insisted on worshipping Yahweh alone, the Christians refused their worship to the new Emperors. They denied them the divine titles which they had begun to usurp. Since for them the word "Lord" had a religious meaning, they would die rather than use it of them. In his *Apology* (Ch. 34) Tertullian[2] set out for us the drama that was still very much a reality in his time. "Augustus," he says, "the creator of the Empire, refused to be addressed as 'Lord'. For, in truth, was this not God's name? For myself, I would willingly call the Emperor 'Lord', but in the ordinary sense, so that the word should not usurp a title that is suitable for God only. For I know myself to be free in relation to the Emperor. My only Lord is the almighty God, who is Lord of the Emperor himself."

We can see in this passage two uses of the word "Lord". One belongs to ordinary life in which "Lord" has a "political" meaning; it is connected with the temporal order and carries no religious significance whatever. Tertullian recognizes that, in this sense, the Emperor is Lord, is his earthly master. But to call the Emperor "Lord" in the sense in which he, Tertullian, calls his God "Lord"—that he refuses absolutely to do. Because of this refusal Christians shed their blood: it was to "Christ the Lord" alone that they sang their hymns "as if to a God". In no way would they consent to put the Roman Emperor and Christ on the same footing. The martyr Donata asserted that "we Christians honour Caesar as Caesar, but it is Christ the Lord whom we reverence and it is to him that our worship is addressed". Was this not the application of Jesus' command to "give back to Caesar what is Caesar's, and to God what is God's" (Mark 12. 17)? To the martyrs, it was Christ Jesus who was "Lord". To him, then, as to the Father, must acclamation and homage be given, to Christ "who rules as God over all things, blessed for ever" (Rom. 9. 5).

The faith of Paul

When the first Christians went to quench their thirst at the spring of St Paul's faith, what did they find in his letters? What did he teach them about Christ, Son of God and Lord, that made them so obstinate in their refusal to call the new

[2] See below, Chapter VI.

Caesars "Lord"? His exposition of his faith on this subject is basically simple. His method—if one can speak of a method in Paul's case—consists in giving to Christ the name that in the Old Testament belonged properly and exclusively to Yahweh: *Lord* or *Adonai*, that is, the all-powerful God to whom all homage belongs. Hence this word is reserved to Jesus; it is his name especially: "for us there is only one God, the Father who is the origin of all things, and the end of our being; only one Lord, Jesus Christ, the creator of all things, who is our way to him" (1 Cor. 8. 6). But his demonstration goes even further: actions whose authorship was, under the old Covenant, rightly attributed to Yahweh, are now credited to Jesus. The following series of texts will illustrate this process:

Yahweh is called "the glorious God" (Ps. 28. 3). But now the risen Christ is "him to whom all glory belongs" (1 Cor. 2. 8). The Lord's thoughts are unsearchable (Isaias 40. 13) but now none can enter into the mind of the Lord (Christ—1 Cor. 2. 16). The Lord owns earth and all earth's fullness, says Psalm 23; St Paul applies this verse to the Lord Jesus (1 Cor. 10. 26).

About salvation Paul declares: "Thou canst find salvation if thou wilt use thy lips to proclaim that Jesus is the Lord, and thy heart to believe that God has raised him up from the dead" (Rom. 10. 9).

We shall find the same assertion in Peter's mouth (Acts 4. 12; see also 3. 6 and 16). But why should salvation spring from this profession of faith? The explanation is to be found in verses 11 and 13. St Paul, in Romans 9. 33, quotes a current version of Isaias 28. 16, "Those who believe in him shall not be disappointed", and it is to this that verse 11 refers.

In Joel 2. 32, we find: "And never a soul shall call on the Lord's name but shall find deliverance." When we find Saul, the Jewish monotheist, the Pharisee well practised in the study and explanation of the Scripture of the old Law, making transpositions of this kind, we can be quite sure that he intends to proclaim the universal Lordship of Christ, and hence his divinity.

Finally, in the great text of Philippians 2. 9–11, Jesus, says St Paul, is given the NAME which is greater than any other

name, and that name is Lord.[3] Perhaps this recalls an ancient
cry of acclamation: "Jesus, Lord", a sort of rallying cry of the
first Christians that included the essential point of their faith
(see 1 Cor. 12. 3, in this connection). So, as formerly every knee
should bow before the Lord Yahweh (Isaias 45. 23) and not
before Baal (3 Kings 19. 18), now it is Jesus Christ who receives supreme adoration from the whole universe: in heaven,
on earth and under the earth.

Jesus will also be proclaimed supreme and universal Judge
when he comes at the world's last day, in a burning fire. St Paul
sets forth his vision of these last events of the Lord's Parousia
or second coming in that great passage of 2 Thessalonians 1. 6
and 12. The interesting thing about this text is that it shows
how the Apostle has put together a brilliant mosaic of those
Old Testament prophecies that foretold the "Day of the Lord",
that is, the judgement which he will mete out to mankind at
the end of time. Transposing these prophecies, St Paul gives
them another subject: through them he describes "the day
when the Lord Jesus appears". This is how the passage is
arranged:

Verse 7.   Jesus will come with fire about him, as was said of
           Yahweh (Isaias 66. 15).
      8.   He will pour out indignation on the nations that do
           not acknowledge God (Jer. 10. 25).
      9.   They will be punished, hiding themselves from the
           Lord's presence (Isaias 2. 10, 19, 21).
     10a. He will come with his saints (Ps. 88. 8).
     10b. Jesus will have his "day", like Yahweh (Isaias 2. 11
           and 17).
     12.   He will be glorified like Yahweh (Isaias 66. 5).

After reading texts like this there could no longer be any
doubt that Jesus was truly God. It is not surprising if Christ

[3] It has been doubted whether this really was St Paul's idea. The
name of Jesus was to be an "unutterable" name. Like Yahweh, who
was no longer referred to by name after the Exile, so that his holiness
might not be profaned, Jesus was to receive a name that none should
know, since none might utter it. But the argument is not decisive, since
the whole trend of the passage seems to be that the Father gives Jesus
the title of "Lord" and the prerogatives that go with it.

is soon to be found at the very centre of the Christian life
and community.

Prayers and worship addressed to Christ the Lord

Faith in the Lord Jesus inspired the primitive community
that had received the Gospel of Christ from Paul and the other
apostles. The firmness of this faith is obvious from the worship
that was given to him and the prayers addressed to him. This
fact struck Pliny the Younger, as we shall see, and the Roman
Festus (Acts 25. 26). These manifestations of faith must next
be examined.

"The Lord is coming", we read in 1 Corinthians 16. 22, and
"Come, Lord Jesus", in Apocalypse 22. 20. The Lord Jesus,
therefore, is awaited by men. His coming will see the end of
the world; he had said it (Matt. 25. 31, 46) and it was accepted.
With faith, hope and love the first Christians awaited him and
prayed to him. They were certain that the "Lord of all Lords,
and King of all Kings" (Apoc. 17. 14; 19. 16) would finally be
victorious over the powers of evil.

They acclaimed and praised him. The "doxologies" we now
use grew from the fervent faith in the Lord of the first Christian
century. (See Rom. 9. 5; 2 Tim. 4. 18; 2 Peter 3. 18; Apoc.
5. 13; 7. 10–12.) They composed hymns in his honour. St Paul
invited the Colossians (3. 16) and the Ephesians (5. 19, 20) to
do so; he even quoted a fragment himself (5. 14):

> Awake, thou that sleepest,
> And rise from the dead,
> And Christ shall give thee light.

In one single verse he gives Timothy a concise summing up
of the life of Jesus:

> Revelation made in human nature,
> justification won in the realm of the Spirit;
> a vision seen by angels,
> a mystery preached to the Gentiles;
> Christ in this world, accepted by faith,
> Christ on high, taken up into glory.
>
> (1 Tim. 3. 16).

In Philippians 2. 6–11, a whole hymn is preserved for us. It sings of the humiliation and exaltation of the Son who becomes "Lord".

Just as we do on the great liturgical feasts, the young community sang the mysteries of our Lord Jesus Christ.

Christ the Lord, the centre of the Christian religion and of the life of the Church

The rôle of redeemer assumed by Jesus would mean nothing if he were not God. The apostles understood this, St Paul especially. If the Father had saved us through the *man* Jesus only it would have been the Father who saved us directly, in the sense that he would have deigned to accept the self-offering that Jesus made to him. But it would not have been the work of him of whom we say with assurance that he is the *Mediator between God and Man*. Jesus saves us by his humanity, through it he is Mediator, but also by the fact that this humanity is that of the Son of God, God himself. This is the basic and ever effective fact on which Christianity is built. It is easy to see this in the Apostle's letters.

Jesus, he says, was "marked out miraculously as the Son of God by his resurrection from the dead" (Rom. 1. 4). Before the Lord every knee must bow (Philipp. 2. 10); even the angels must adore him (Hebrews 1. 6, but read the whole chapter). It is useless, then, to place faith anywhere but in him. At the time when the Apostle was writing, false teachers were spreading corrupt doctrines. It was thought that the heavenly bodies were alive and had the ordering of this world. People placed their hope in these celestial beings and believed that, as a whole, they constituted a plenitude, a "pleroma" of power. But St Paul peremptorily undeceived the Christians: it is in Jesus Christ, he wrote to the Colossians (2. 9–10), that "the whole plenitude of the Deity is embodied, and dwells in him, and it is in him that you find your completion; he is the fountain-head from which all dominion and power proceed".

Why look elsewhere for support when in Christ is our whole life? Christ is our head as a consequence of his Lordship, the title that indicates his position in the spiritual life of men. He has become the head of mankind by his glorious resurrection, he continues in his Church the work which he began in the Creation: "he takes precedence of all, and in him all subsist. He too is that head whose body is the Church; it begins with him, since his was the first birth out of death; thus in every way the primacy was to become his. It was God's good pleasure to let all completeness dwell in him" (Col. 1. 17–19). The expression "in Christ Jesus", which is common in Paul's writings, draws all its force from this text of Colossians. It reminds us that our salvation, in all its completeness, comes to us by the man-God, the Lord Jesus, "the great God . . . our Saviour Jesus Christ" (Titus 2. 13–14).

Christ, the centre of the Church, must also be the axis of the Christian life. In teaching us that our vocation is to be moulded into the image of the Son (Rom. 8. 29), St Paul reveals to us the secret of our relationship with God: we are "sons in the Son". One text is enough to show this: "Then God sent out his Son on a mission to us. He took birth from a woman, took birth as a subject of the Law, so as to ransom those who were subject to the Law and make us sons by adoption. To prove that you are sons, God has sent out the Spirit of his Son into our hearts, crying out in us, Abba, Father. No longer, then, art thou a slave, thou art a son; and because thou art a son thou hast a son's right of inheritance" (Gal. 4. 4–7).

THE HOLY SPIRIT

The Person who is known to us nowadays as the third Person of the Blessed Trinity is given less space in St Paul's writings than the Son and Lord; but this does not make him any the less important. Once again, St Paul speaks of him in a practical way. The mission of the Holy Spirit can be summed up in this way: he brings to the faithful the life of God and of Christ. He is the sanctifying Spirit whose personal activity is parallel to that of Father and Son, but different from theirs. His rôle and his work are so well defined that we feel at once that it is no longer a question merely of a divine activity as in the Old Testament: he is a Person, a being who can be addressed, to whom divine qualities are ascribed. Christians are purified, sanctified, justified, "in the name of the Lord Jesus, by the Spirit of the God we serve" (1 Cor. 6. 11). The Trinitarian form of this verse puts the Spirit on the same level as the Lord Jesus (see also Titus 3. 6).

The body of a Christian has its own high dignity: it is the Temple of the Holy Spirit (1 Cor. 6.19). For this reason alone St Paul begs the Corinthians no longer to indulge in debauchery, for it is a sin against the body whose guest is the Holy Spirit. This reminder was certainly worth more than all the moral exhortations to which, unfortunately, we have too often become accustomed.

We are given the assurance that the Kingdom of God will be established by rightness of heart (that is, by God's life), peace and joy in the Holy Spirit (Rom. 14. 17). It is the Holy Spirit who pours out the love of God in our hearts (Rom. 5. 5). But the word of the Gospel of Jesus is proclaimed to the Gentiles so that, sanctified by the Holy Spirit, they may become an offering worthy of acceptance; it is this that brings most joy to the Father (Rom. 15. 15). We can compare this text with certain passages in the Acts, such as 10. 44–8.

To live in the Holy Spirit—this is another Pauline expression. It is often used in parallel to the one we noticed above— "in Christ Jesus". "Justification", that is, the passage from sin to the life of God, comes either through Christ (Gal. 2. 17), or by Christ and the Holy Spirit (1 Cor. 6. 11). Sanctification is in Christ Jesus (1 Cor. 1. 2) or in the Holy Spirit (Rom. 15. 16).

Is there no contradiction in this? We must make no mistake about it. St Paul uses the expressions "in Christ" and "in the Spirit" indifferently because both bring us sanctification, though in different ways. When he speaks of *ransoming* and *saving* men, then it is Christ whose merits have gained their sanctification and salvation. He it is who has merited this. To live in Christ means, in this case, to live by the grace which he obtained by ransoming us (1 Cor. 6. 20) and which should lead us to imitate his life (Gal. 2. 19–20). But the glorified Christ has sent the Holy Spirit, who is his Spirit (Rom. 8. 9). In the ages to come and in the Church it is he who will communicate to us the life of God (1 Cor. 6. 11). It can truly be said then, that the Spirit brings us God's gifts, and a beautiful passage which St Paul wrote to the Corinthians as a subject on which they should reflect, assures us of it. The action of the Holy Spirit is placed alongside that of Father and Son. All three work together for our salvation, but each in his own way (1 Cor. 12. 4–11).

This passage concerns "charismata", or extraordinary spiritual favours, which enabled certain members of the Christian community to speak several languages, to prophesy, to work miracles and so on. They knew that these favours were a gift of the Spirit. No one must boast of these gifts or "charismata", says the Apostle, for "all this is the work of one and the same Spirit, who distributes his gifts as he will to each severally" (verse 11). But these gifts are not attributed to the Holy Spirit alone, but also to the Father and the Son, though in different ways. Coming from the Holy Spirit, they are "charismata" or spiritual gifts, an enduring possession, a kind of spiritual riches. But seen in relation to the Lord, these gifts are "kinds of service", that is, tasks apportioned by Christ to assist in building the Church. In other words, since the Lord's work was to build up this body, and since this was his especial task, the gifts that the Holy Spirit bestows on us lay on the Christian a task which is the continuation of Christ's (Ephes. 4. 11–12). Finally, in relation to the Father, these gifts are "manifestations of power", activities bearing fruit in the Church. Certainly the Father is at the origin of all things, he is the source of all effective activity, the One whose action is all in all. For St Paul, then, the Trinity of divine persons may be set out as follows:

> The Father, origin of all, source of activity, sends
> by the ministry of the Son, who is the source of merit,
> the Holy Spirit, who distributes the gifts that have been won.

So each one works together at building the Church, and each in his own way gives life to the Christian, assigning him his place in the apostolate. Later on Christian faith and piety were to recall this in the development of the Church's worship.

THE TRINITY IS OUR SALVATION

Our final reading from St Paul requires us to widen our range of vision. We are attempting to take in all the work of the Trinity at a glance, and the eighth chapter of the Epistle to the Romans makes it possible in a few verses to cover the work of the three Persons in us. This chapter recapitulates the whole trinitarian theology of St Paul, and at the same time it is, one might say, the "guide to habitual grace". But it is a living thing, for grace, here, is the Persons in us. Following this train of thought:

1. In order to condemn sin, the Father sends his own Son (3, 32).
   The Holy Spirit is *his* Spirit (9, 11, 14).
   The Father is also *our* Father (11, 21, 28, 30).
2. The Son is sent by the Father (3, 32),
   to ransom creation (19, 22–3).
   The Holy Spirit is *his* Spirit also (9—see also Gal. 4. 6).
3. The Holy Spirit is the Spirit of Father and Son (9, 11, 14).
   He is the principal of life in Christians. It is necessary to be indwelt by him in order to belong to God and to Christ (9, 14; see 5. 5).
   He makes us heirs with Christ (16–17).
   He makes us feel that we are adopted sons, since he makes us call God "Father" (15). In Galatians 4. 6, it is he who cries "Father" in our hearts.
   It is he who assures us that we are sons (16). It is he who comes to the aid of our weakness, interceding for us with groans unutterable, for we do not know what prayer to offer, to pray as we ought (26).
   But he does so according to the mind of God (27).

So spoke St Paul to the Churches. But the Apostle's message still has force and value to re-create "live" Christians in the twentieth century. Apart from Father, Son and Holy Spirit there can be no real Christian life, for they are its source. We are called to live with them. Saturated with the divine life which is communicated to them by the Spirit, Christians will always find an answer to the burning questions that face them. The letters of St Paul have been sufficient to resolve difficulties as great as our own.

One last text shall conclude this study of St Paul's theology, casting on it a final ray of light. In the closing greeting that Paul adds in his own handwriting to a letter to his beloved Corinthians, he writes: "The grace of our Lord Jesus Christ, and the love of God, and the imparting of the Holy Spirit be with you" (2 Cor. 13. 13).

"The *grace* of our Lord Jesus Christ"—this is an habitual formula in Paul's greetings (see 1 Cor. 16. 23; Gal. 6. 8; Philipp. 4. 23). It is a reminder of a constant and essential part of his teaching: grace comes from our Lord Jesus Christ who won our redemption and salvation (Rom. 3. 24–5). That is what the Apostle wishes for them.

"The love of God" (the Father), because the Father is its source. This love is absolutely free: it is entirely a gift, entirely disinterested. It recalls an idea that St Paul was fond of: the Father loved us before we loved him, even when we were still sinners (Rom. 8. 3, 32, 39); this is the foundation of our absolute trust in him (Rom. 5. 8–9). It is a specially Christian love: it is called "agape", a love of goodwill freely given, as opposed to "eros", the love of which the Greek philosophers spoke, the desire to possess, man reaching out towards that which is his joy and his end. The Greeks never grasped the meaning of divine "agape". Their gods sometimes had "eros" for men, and they were always on their side the objects of "eros", but it was a powerless "eros".

In St Paul's eyes God has no "eros" for a creature which is powerless to enrich him; he alone is the source of "agape". St John tells us that he himself is "agape" (1 John 4. 8).

"The *imparting* of the Holy Spirit", because he is the agent of our communion with one another, by means of the love that he brings into our hearts (Rom. 5. 5), a love whose nature it is to draw beings together to unite them and to make them alike. The love given by the Spirit aims at uniting all Christians, all men, by making them like God.

This is our one chance of salvation, says St Paul: the *grace* of our Lord Jesus Christ, the *love* of God, and the *fellowship* that he creates by the Spirit. The message is there for us to read.

CHAPTER IV

THE REVELATION OF THE
TRINITY IN ST JOHN

THE SPIRIT OF ST JOHN

The Christ of St Paul is a spiritual Christ, risen and glorious. The Christ of St John is primarily the person he knew in the flesh, the one who, when they first met, said to Andrew and almost certainly to John himself, "Come and see" (1. 39).[1] So it was a man, the man Jesus, whom John first knew. The meeting on the river bank is the opposite of that on the road to Damascus. There, it was the divine Christ, resplendent in glory; here, a simple meeting with a stranger in whom no trace of divine glory could be discerned. But John was to pierce the mystery of the young teacher by the river bank. His whole Gospel was written to pass on to us the message of this Man who had come to reveal God: "No man has ever seen God; but now his only-begotten Son, who abides in the bosom of the Father, has himself become our interpreter" (1. 18). His whole soul was deeply marked by the mystery that the Master unfolded when he announced himself as God's messenger, sent to reveal him, nothing less than the sign of his presence among men.

[1] All references in this chapter are to St John's Gospel unless other-wise stated.

St John, then, wrote his Gospel with well-defined intentions. Rather than merely completing the message of the synoptic Gospels, John wanted to send his own message to Christians whose faith was in danger. For by the end of the first century two errors had found their way into the infant Church. The first denied that Christ was truly God: this was the error of Gnosticism. The second was that of Docetism which denied that Christ was truly man.[2] That is why, throughout his Gospel, St John asserts that Jesus is God and that his actions and words force us to recognize this. The Prologue (1. 1–18), written after the event, is there to reinforce the demonstration. All this is perhaps only of indirect interest to us, but it does help us to understand St John's purpose better when he speaks of Jesus, true man and true God, revelation of the Father, and cause of the sending of the Holy Spirit.

THE FATHER, SOURCE OF SALVATION, GLORIFIED BY JESUS

Here as in St Paul, the Father's own name is often *God*. St John tells us that he is invisible but revealed by Jesus (1. 18). His is the name that Jesus has come to make known to men (17. 6), and none may know him unless Jesus makes him known (5. 31–8).

The Father is he who never ceases to work (5. 17), it is he on whom Jesus models himself (5. 19–20), from him he derives his powers (5. 21–30; 20. 21).

Again, the Father is the *source* of salvation: impelled by love he sends his Son to save us (3. 16). That is why St John gives him the name, Love.

God (that is the Father) is love. The revelation of the love of God, where we are concerned, is in the sending of his only-begotten Son into the world so that we might have life through him (1 John. 4. 8–9).

The Father is the *end* as well as the source of salvation. As in St Paul's writings it is towards him that all things tend. The work of Christ is to *interpret* the Father (1. 18), but eternal

[2] See Vols. 24 and 136.

life is to know him, and Jesus Christ whom he has sent (17. 3). The end of Jesus' discourse and prayer sums up the aim of his mission: "I have revealed, and will reveal, thy name to them; so that the love thou hast bestowed upon me may dwell in them, and I, too, may dwell in them" (17. 26).

Again as in St Paul, the work of Christ seems to be less the salvation of men than the glorification of the Father by their salvation (17. 26).

THE SON, WORD AND WITNESS OF GOD

The Latin *verbum* gives us our "word", and this is a translation of the Greek λόγος which is used by St John alone.

The idea of the Word of God in St John is both original and peculiarly his own. Never before had anyone spoken of a Word existing in God as a living personality, before appearing among men in their very nature. Neither the Greeks, in the natural theology in which they described the birth of the gods and of the world, not even Philo, a Jewish theologian and philosopher who was a contemporary of Jesus Christ, had thought of God as "living" to the extent of expressing himself in an eternal Word, one which we know to be a Person. St John's boldness, then, lay in his application to the Son of God of the teaching that the Old Testament writers gave on the subject of the "word of God". But there it was simply a divine act. Now the Evangelist tells us that it is the Son of God, incarnate for our salvation. Here again St John's theological intuition is only equalled by that of St Paul who identified the "Wisdom" and "Image" of God with the Person of Christ himself.

St John uses the term "Word" six times: four times in the Prologue, once in the first Epistle, once in the Apocalypse.

In the first verse of his Gospel he uses it three times: "At the beginning of time the Word already was; and God had the Word abiding with him, and the Word was God."

St John emphasizes first that the Word existed before creatures: "At the beginning of time the Word already was", he existed when things were created. The Word had no beginning.

This contrasts him with creatures, which do have a beginning. This first verse of St John is designed to make clear the difference between the Word and creatures, of whom the first verse of Genesis tells us that they were created at the beginning of time: "God, at the beginning of time, created heaven and earth." Also the Word is in a privileged position: he was with God before the world was made. Further, he is God. This makes clear to us his nature and his transcendence.

Verse 3 insists on this: the Word not only existed before the world, but the universe itself was made by him, it owes its being to him. At one stroke St John takes us far beyond the reach of imagination: the Word is the universal cause of all that exists, nothing escapes his creative action.

The verses that follow emphasize this still further. The Word is presented to us as possessing the same qualities as the Father. The Father is Life and Light (1 John 1. 7; 5. 11), so also is the Word (1 John 4. 9).

Verse 14 gives us the fourth use of "Word". The previous verses concern the state of the Word before his Incarnation: even in the Old Testament he enlightened every soul (1. 9), in fact it is to him that St John attributes the theophanies.[3] But the Word did more: he was made flesh and came to dwell among us, in order to bring us *grace*, which is the possession of God's life, and *truth*, which is his Revelation. It is he who is now known to us under the name of Jesus, Son of God.

In the first verse of his first Epistle St John again uses this expression, but here he is the "Word who is life", for he is the one who gives it, as the Gospel says (1. 16).

Finally the Apocalypse (19. 12–13) shows us a vision of a rider on a white horse: "On his brow were many royal diadems; the name written there is one that only he knows. He went clad in a garment deep dyed with blood, and the name by which he is called is the Word of God."

He is presented to us in the guise of a judge: with his two-

---

[3] See John 8. 56. The Greek Fathers said later that the Word came among men when God manifested himself in the Old Testament. St Irenaeus explained that he was getting used to the habits of this world and so preparing for his Incarnation!

edged sword, the symbol of the destroying word as we saw in
the book of Wisdom (18. 16), he will annihilate the nations
that oppose him. For this reason, his victory is signified by
another name, "King of Kings and Lord of Lords," and the
image of the sword is made clearer by that of the blood in
which his tunic is soaked.

Son of God equal to the Father—such, then, is the Word of
God. He existed before creation; he is a person distinct from
the Father, but he shares his power as creator, Saviour, and
judge of the world. The "Word of God" has truly become a
Person who acts: he creates, reveals, saves, judges. We can
see why at Christmas time the Church makes us re-read, with
a joy that springs from seeing it in the light of the incarnation
of the Word of God, the magnificent passage of Wisdom
(18. 14–16). Nothing can give us a better starting-point for our
meditation on the Word of God in St John than to re-read
these verses from the new point of view which we have now
gained.

THE PERSON OF JESUS: THE GOD-MAN AS WITNESS TO THE FATHER

One feature above all distinguishes Jesus as he is shown in
St John's Gospel: he is equal to the Father. It is with the
powerful presentation of him given by the Prologue in our
minds that we are to consider the text of the body of the
Gospel. St John says so with emphasis: "So much has been
written down that you may learn to believe Jesus is the Christ,
the Son of God, and so believing find life through his name"
(20. 31).

Jesus, then, is the Son of God, Son in a special way (5. 19, 22;
20. 17). He has the same power as the Father: "My Father has
never ceased working and I too must be at work" (5. 17). He
knows all secrets (3. 11–13) because they come to him from
the Father (8. 23–8). His action and his knowledge are parallel
to those of the Father, therefore he is his equal, God himself.

At the same time—this is the second feature of this Gospel
—Jesus remains dependent upon the Father. It is from him that
he has received all that he is: "As the Father has within him

the gift of life, so he has granted to the Son that he too should have within him the gift of life" (5. 26). The Father "has given everything into his hands" (3. 35). In his work also this dependence is preserved (8. 28; 5. 19–22).

This dependence of the Son is the basis of his mission from the Father. We saw this first of all in the Old Testament. St John was convinced that it was the Word, hence the Son, who was manifested to the patriarchs. Chapter 8. 56 is an allusion to Genesis 17. 15–17, and 18. Chapter 12. 41 refers explicitly to Isaias 6. 1–6.

Better still, Jesus has come among us as a saviour and it is the Father's love that has contrived this mission (3. 16; see also 5.3 and 6; and 1 John 4. 9). Also Jesus' coming had a clearly defined goal which determined the part that he was to play: Jesus was to make known the Father (1. 18; 17. 6), to declare his glory, his sovereign perfection (17. 4). Yet in spite of his position of "envoy", we must not suppose that Jesus became in any way inferior to the Father. If he declares "my Father has greater power than I" (14. 28), it is because the Father, we feel, is still the very mystery of God, the one whom none has seen nor can see save through the Son and through his work (14. 9 and 8. 19). The legate appears inferior to the one who sent him, and yet if he did not share his nature he could not accomplish his mission. Jesus is sent by the Father, but he holds all things equally with the Father (16. 15) and his actions are truly those of God. They are summed up in those specifically divine gifts—the grace and truth which he brings us (1. 17).

THE HOLY SPIRIT, SOURCE OF TRUTH AND LIFE

By the same right as the Son, the Holy Spirit in St John's writings possesses a divine activity. But what the Son is to the Father, the Holy Spirit is to the Son. The Son has exalted the Father's glory (17. 4), the Holy Spirit will bring honour to the Son (16. 14). The Son has made the Father known (17. 6), the Holy Spirit will make known the Son. In other words he will make us understand the revelation which we have been given (14. 26; 15. 26; 16. 14–15).

Finally, the Holy Spirit is the soul of the Church. Now that Jesus is risen and glorified he gives her life: "On the last and greatest day of the feast Jesus stood there and cried aloud, If any man is thirsty let him come to me and drink; yes, if a man believes in me as the scripture says, Fountains of living water shall flow from his bosom. He was speaking here of the Spirit which was to be received by those who learned to believe in him—the Spirit which had not yet been given to men because Jesus had not yet been raised to glory" (7. 37–9).

So the Spirit is that living water that flows from the pierced side of Jesus, and it is given to the Church now that Jesus is in glory. These verses are extremely helpful in giving us the right point of view in our meditations on the gift of Jesus to his Church. The Messias had already announced it to the Samaritan woman under the symbol of living water (4. 14). Sacramental theology draws some of its most important conclusions from this symbolism, by relating Christian rites to the pierced side of Christ, to the Lord in glory and to the Holy Spirit, the source of living water.

Although this text comes to us from another hand than that which gave us the Acts of the Apostles, it puts before us, in perfect harmony with it, the vivid story of the first Christian achievements.

THE GREAT REVELATION OF THE TRINITY

It is not only recently that Chapters 14 to 16 of St John have attracted the attention of commentators. They have noticed that in this last conversation with his friends the Master perfected the revelation of the Trinity. St Gregory Nazianzen remarked that there was even a progression in the revelation of the three Persons.

We select here four texts in which this progression is particularly apparent and in which the rôle of the three Persons is most clearly expressed.

"I will ask the Father, and he will give you another to befriend you, one who is to dwell continually with you for ever. It is the truth-giving Spirit, for whom the world can find no

room, because it cannot see him, cannot recognize him"
(14. 16–17).

Jesus will pray to the Father, and at his request "another"
will be sent to dwell for ever among the faithful, with them
and in them.

"He who is to befriend you, the Holy Spirit, whom the
Father will send on my account will in his turn make everything plain, and recall to your minds everything I have said
to you" (14. 26).

The Father will send the Holy Spirit for Jesus' sake. The
purpose of this mission is revealed: to make Jesus' message
clear, because until then it had been unintelligible to the
Apostles. This is very revealing: it is useless to try to find the
whole message in the words of Jesus by themselves. The truth
is all there, but only as the stream is in its source. This source
must be tapped by the Church in which it becomes a great
river, thanks to the Holy Spirit who was promised and sent for
this purpose. Without him the words of Jesus would be a dead
letter, without further development, unfruitful. *With* him, the
group of the apostles, and undoubtedly also their successors
throughout history—since the mission of the Spirit was not
confined to the time of the Church's foundation—possess what
we now call the gift of infallibility in interpreting the words
of Jesus.

In Chapter 15. 26, Jesus says: "When he, the truth-giving
Spirit, who proceeds from the Father, has come to befriend
you, he whom I will send to you from the Father's side, he will
bear witness of what I was."

Here, it is Jesus himself who sends the Spirit, still in order
to bear witness to him, so that we also may know and bear
witness in our turn. It is clear also that when the Spirit has
given us knowledge of the Son and brought us into close friendship with him, we shall find in it knowledge of the Father,
since to know the Son is to know the Father (14. 9–10).

We can follow this wonderful train of thought: the Father
sends the Son; when the Son is in glory he prays to the Father
to send the Spirit, or even he himself sends him. The Spirit,
then, comes from the Father, through the Son. But in his turn

the Spirit brings us to the knowledge of the Son, which is life in him, so that, brought into the nuptial chamber of the Bridegroom, we come at last to the loving knowledge of the Father. So once more we come back to him.

Finally, Jesus says that the condition of the coming of the Spirit is that he himself should go away (16. 7–15). It is necessary that he should go back to his Father so that he may send him to us. The Spirit, he says again, will bring us into truth, making known to the Church and murmuring in the souls of the faithful all that he has learnt in the heart of the Trinity: what he will proclaim is what he has received, Jesus himself.

It is a wonderful discourse, a moment of fullest communion between Jesus and his friends. It plunges us into the depths of God. St John tells us about the relationship between the Three: the Father is in the Son and the Son in the Father (10. 30; 14. 11 and 20), but the Spirit also is in them since from them comes all that he teaches us (16. 15). But St John also makes us realize the way in which Father, Son and Holy Spirit are all deeply involved in the story of our salvation; they turn towards us to bring life to our souls. In this world the Blessed Trinity becomes light and holiness.

This same plan of God the Three-in-One is evoked once more by that last vivid picture in the Apocalypse (22. 1). The Angel shows St John a river whose waters give life; it flows, clear as crystal, "from the throne of God, from the throne of the Lamb". This river is the Spirit of holiness which flows from the Father and the Son. It is the living water that Jesus promised to the Samaritan woman so that she might quench her soul's thirst. It is the mysterious water that John saw flowing from the pierced side of Christ on the cross, but here both Father and Son are its source. On the feast of Pentecost the Church still prays in the *Veni, Creator Spiritus*, that it may come to us:

> *Accende lumen sensibus,*
> *Infunde amorem cordibus . . .*
> O guide our minds with thy blest light,
> With love our hearts inflame.

*   *   *

It is time to finish our reading of Scripture and conclude this first part of the book.

With the Synoptists, the Acts, with St Paul and St John, we have penetrated into the mystery of God. We have read their texts unhurriedly, seeking to find in them only what had been placed there by the sacred authors, but also to find in them all that they wished them to contain. We have been enlightened by what we have received from their living instruction. From now on the Old and New Testaments are not entirely closed books to us, for we have encountered in them a little of the mystery of God. The Spirit of Jesus has shown us their meaning. But our task is not finished: twenty centuries of Christian thought remain to be explored. What has the Spirit been able to reveal to the Church of Christ during that time? The second and third parts of this book will tell us. In the second part we shall see heresy give rise to speculation. Faced with error, the faith of the first Christian teachers sought the truth, worked out a living "catechesis",[4] prayed and bore witness to the truth. "Professions of faith", or *creeds*, spread throughout the Church. Christians lived by this faith and died for it. But the rule of their prayer became that of their faith; the Three-in-One was a living God to them.

In the third part our reflections will be guided by the conclusions of teachers like St Augustine and St Thomas Aquinas. The struggles to defend the faith, the efforts to clarify it, are no longer necessary. But it is necessary for us to come to rest in the very heart of God. Reason will lead us there. "I *believe* that God is Three-in-One" becomes, still very humbly, "I *know* God, the Three-in-One", I know what he is in himself and I see, through him, what man is, formed in his image.

[4] Catechesis, methodical instruction on the truths of salvation.

P A R T I I

THE CHRISTIAN CREEDS

I praise thee (Father), I bless thee,
I glorify thee, through the eternal and
heavenly High Priest
Jesus Christ, thy beloved child, through
whom be glory to thee
with him and with the Holy Spirit
now and in the ages to come.

Amen.

(Martyrdom of St Polycarp 14. 3.)

ORIGINS OF THE PRINCIPAL TRINITARIAN HERESIES AND THEIR REFUTATION

I. *TOTAL REJECTION OF THE TRINITY*

	HERESY		REFUTATION		
Year	Of Judaizing Origin	Of Philosophical Origin	Inspired Writers	Final Authority	Christian Teachers
50	Ebionites.	Simon Magus	St Paul.	T h e A p o s t l e s' C R E E D	St Clement of Rome (96–100).
100	Cerinthus (96–100).	Basilides. Valentine.	St John.		St Ignatius of Antioch (†107).
150		Marcion.			St. Justin (150).
200		(Widespread Gnosticism).			St Irenaeus.

II. *REJECTION OF THE DISTINCTION OF PERSONS*

	HERESY		REFUTATION	
Year	Adoptionism	Modalism	Teachers	Final Authority
200	Theodotus the Currier. Theodotus the Banker. Artemon.	Praxeas.	Tertullian (213–18).	
250	Paul of Samosata. (The Word lives in the man Jesus as in a Temple. Hence Jesus is not the Son of God.)	Sabellius. Noëtus of Smyrna.	Hippolytus of Rome (c.230–40).	The two Denises (265). The Three Councils of Antioch (263–8).

III. *REJECTION OF EQUALITY OF PERSONS*

	ERRORS		REFUTATION	
Year	About the Word	About the Holy Spirit	Teachers	Final Authority
300	Arius. Eusebius of Nicomedia. Eusebius of Caesarea.		St Alexander of Alexandria (320). St Athanasius. St Hilary.	Nicea (325).
350	Anomeans. Homoi-ousians. Homoeans.	Pneumato-machians. Macedonius.	St Athanasius. St Basil of Caesarea. St Gregory of Nyssa.	Alexandria (362).
400		Marathon.	St Gregory Nazianzen.	2nd Council of Constanti-nople (381).

CHAPTER V

THE SECOND CENTURY

FIRST HERESIES,[1] FIRST STRUGGLES

Faith in the Trinity was magnificently expressed by St Paul and St John. The faithful had no need to look elsewhere for the nourishment of their faith and love. All the same, serious difficulties remained which were not long in making themselves felt. The pattern of life and thought in the second century gave them a foothold.

First of all there was the Jewish religious climate. Faith in the Trinity could not but collide with that of the Jews, bound as they were with every fibre of their being to the one God. It was evident from the beginning that a large section of the Jewish milieu could not accept this new dogma which seemed to impair their notion of one God. The difficulty immediately crystallized around the person of Jesus. It was necessary to explain the mystery of his coming, life, words and actions. In this negative current we first encounter as early as St Paul's time people called Ebionites, that is, etymologically, "the poor". They were faithful to the law of Moses, and had no intention of going beyond the revelation of the nature of the one God that had been handed down to them. Later, at the end of the century, when St John was writing, there appeared at Ephesus a Jewish doctor from Alexandria, called Cerinthus. He came to that city in order to oppose the faith brought there by St Paul.

[1] Heresy: an error which strikes at the root of the Church's faith, at one of the main articles of the Creed. See Volumes 4 and 136 in this series.

The Ebionites and Cerinthus, holding fast to their faith in the one God, suggested that Jesus was not God, that we should see him as an ordinary man, the son of Joseph and Mary. They were ready to admit that he was the promised Messias, and Cerinthus claimed that at Jesus' baptism in Jordan a heavenly spirit whose name was *Christ* entered into him to charge him with the special mission of proclaiming the Father. In any case, Jesus was not truly God, but the Messias or a prophet.

Along with these first heretics, too faithfully submissive to the old revelation, there were others no less dangerous, who wanted to reconcile the Jewish and Christian faiths with philosophy. These were the "Gnostics".

Already in St Paul's time—the Acts of the Apostles (8. 9–10) tells us about it—a certain Simon, a magician by profession, had made a great impression on the people of Samaria. He proclaimed himself "the great angel of God," that is, a man inhabited by a heavenly spirit as Jesus had been. His fame was so great that everyone followed him.

But more formidable and more complex were the errors of those known to history as Basilides, Valentine and Marcion between the years 100 and 150. They taught a doctrine about God that was subtle, the more so in that it consisted in a combination of several different beliefs. These men were Jews, hence they would not abandon the divine unity. On the other hand, a certain brand of neo-Platonic and gnostic philosophy formed the foundation of their education. This philosophy taught them that matter and the body are essentially evil things of which a good and spiritual God could never have been the author. Who, then, could have made the material world but those spiritual beings called "aeons", something between matter and God, but quite inferior to God who is pure spirit? And to crown this iniquity, not only had an "aeon" created matter, but one of them had imprisoned in it a spark of light, which should be the possession of the spiritual world alone. Who would set it free? The third element, Christianity, offered a solution. A divine "aeon" had entered into Jesus and united itself to him. Why? In order to make a *Saviour* of him. Not that Jesus had ransomed the evil corporeal world by his passion and resurrection. Since he was not God he was powerless to do so. The rôle of Jesus was to offer to mankind a higher knowledge, the "gnosis" or knowledge of the ways of salvation. These ways consisted in achieving detachment from matter in order to become purely spiritual.

Such doctrines tended to empty the mystery of God of all meaning. Salvation was no more than an escape, and man could reach it alone by following Christ's example, without the help of grace. Moreover, it is noticeable that the interest centred on the person of Jesus and the Holy Spirit had no place in these speculations.

FIRST STRUGGLES IN DEFENCE OF THE THREE-IN-ONE

The inspired teachers

Once again we find St Paul ready for battle. At Colossae and at Ephesus he was already struggling against the "Judaizers" in order to anchor the faith on Christ, the Son of God.

St Paul explained to the Colossians (1. 15–20) that Christ is the "likeness" of God, the cause and head of all things, for in him there is a "pleroma", or completeness, so that in him all things are summed up and "recapitulated": completeness is to be understood in the sense that since the Father has placed all things in him, Christ is the synthesis of divinity, of the heavenly Powers, of the whole Universe that he has created, and of the whole ransomed Church. Hence he is equal to God, superior to all and every heavenly spirit; he is above the "elements of this world" who were the spiritual beings believed to uphold the universe.

In the following chapter, verses 4–10, St Paul tells them that "the whole plenitude of the Deity is embodied" in Christ, that is, in his human nature. So all "philosophizing" apart from him is false. There is nothing to be found apart from Christ, the head of all "Princedoms" and of all "Dominions".[2] He has

[2] These expressions refer to the categories of "angels"—the spiritual beings in whom the Colossians put all their faith and trust (see Ephes. 1).

power enough to triumph over all evil "powers", all fallen angels.

The other inspired teacher is St John. His opponents were both "Docetists" and "Gnostics".[3] Against the latter his task was to show that Jesus is true God. We are reminded of the Prologue, which was written to oppose them and to confirm the faith of the first Christians. The creative Word is perfect God. Jesus is the Word, hence Jesus is God.

Some Christian teachers

The struggle was not over. At the beginning of the second century we find the holy Bishop Ignatius of Antioch (he who was to die a martyr's death, ground by the teeth of wild beasts), returning to it.[4] When he wrote to the Romans of the sufferings which he was to undergo at Rome, he described to them his joy at the thought of "imitating the passion of his God" (*To the Romans*, 6. 3). Where could we find a more magnificent profession of faith?

To the Ephesians he addressed a warning against false teachers. Jesus, he said, experienced two states: he was born of Mary as a healer, for the sake of our salvation, and in this capacity he was begotten according to the flesh, with a capacity to suffer, but he is also "unbegotten"; by this Ignatius means true God.

> Men of perverse cunning speak everywhere in God's name, but they act otherwise and in a manner unworthy of God: you must avoid them as you would wild beasts. They are mad dogs who bite on the sly. You must be on your guard against them, for their bites are hard to cure. There is but one doctor, both fleshly and spiritual, begotten and unbegotten; made flesh, yet God; in death true life; born of Mary and born of God; first passible and now impassible: Jesus Christ our Lord (*To the Ephesians* 7 1–2).

But Ignatius does not know God the Son alone, he can speak also of the three Persons. In a wonderful way he makes the

---

[3] See Part I, Chapter IV.

[4] St Ignatius of Antioch died a martyr at Rome in 107. He wrote seven letters which are precious examples of ancient Christian literature. He is known as one of the Apostolic Fathers.

Trinity the model of every human community. To the Magnesians he writes:

> Take care to be strong in the teaching of the Lord and his apostles, so that all that you do may succeed [Ps. 1. 3] in flesh and spirit, in faith and charity, in the Son, the Father and the Spirit, in the beginning and at the end, with your most worthy bishop and the precious spiritual crown of your priests and with your holy deacons. Submit to the bishop and to each other [St Paul, Ephes. 5. 21] as Christ in the flesh submitted to the Father and the Spirit, so that the union may be both of the flesh and of the Spirit. (*To the Magnesians* 13. 2.)

Finally there is the great passage in which he ranges himself beside St Paul against the false teachers, at the same time giving us a glimpse of the mystery of our return to God:

> I have heard that certain people coming from there had been among you, bringing false doctrine; but you did not allow them to sow their seed among you; you stopped your ears so as not to receive what they sow, in the thought that you are the stones of the Father's temple, prepared for building by God the Father, raised to the right height by that machine of Jesus Christ which is the cross, by means of the cable which is the Holy Spirit.

St Justin,[5] the second teacher whom we must consider, is doubly interesting, for he spoke of the mystery of God as much to the Jews as to the pagans. His method, founded on discussion of the basis of his faith and its justification, has caused him to be counted among the Apologists.

Justin's first work was his *Dialogue* with Tryphon the Jew, who was another of those who denied the Trinity. He set out to demonstrate that the coming of Jesus is not contrary to the holy Scriptures of the Old Testament in which Tryphon believed. Was it not the Word who had already been manifested to the Patriarchs, thus anticipating his Incarnation by coming among men? Certainly the expressions that Justin used are not always very exact. For example he declared that it would

[5] A Christian teacher in Rome, Justin died a martyr about 165–6. He had been converted to Christianity. Tired of all the philosophies because he could find in them no answers to the mysteries of man and of evil, Christianity seemed to him the only way to enlightenment.

not be fitting for the Father to become incarnate. From this he concludes: "It follows that we must believe that inferior to the Creator of the universe there is another God and Lord who is called 'angel',[6] because he announces to men whatever is given him to announce by the Creator of the universe, above whom is no other God" (*Dialogue*, 61).

Christ seems to be placed below the Father, who is God preeminently. But what Justin is saying here is above all that the Father is invisible, and that he needed a messenger in order to make himself known.

St Justin also wrote two *Apologies*, addressed to the philosopher-Emperor, Marcus Aurelius. He explains very cleverly that he, the Emperor, a Stoic philosopher, believes in a "seminal word", that is a sort of "germ" from which the universe came forth. Having got so far, he will more easily give a hearing to an explanation that the Word of God is analogous to this, and that the world found its origin in him.

On the other hand, since the accusations flung at the Christians went to the lengths of accusing them of atheism (because Christians refused to sacrifice to the pagan gods), he drew up a statement of his faith in the God in whom he believed:

> We are not heretics, we who venerate the Creator of the Universe. . . . And we will show you also that we are right to honour the one who taught us this doctrine and who was begotten for that purpose, Jesus Christ, who was crucified under Pontius Pilate governor of Judaea in the time of the Caesar Tiberius; we have been taught to recognize in him the Son of the true God, and him we put in the second place, and in the third place we put the prophetic Spirit (*First Apology* 13. 1–3).

Still a very clumsy theology, but one which made it possible to answer the opponents of the Christian faith. The transcendence of God the Father led inevitably to the idea of rank in the Trinity, the Son being in the second place and the Holy Spirit in the third. Also, St Justin seemed to say that the Word of God only acquired independence and personal reality by coming into this world, in the Creation or the Incarnation. But

[6] An allusion to the prophet Malachias, 3. 1. "Angel" is used in the sense of "messenger".

what concerned St Justin above all, while affirming the reality
of the three Persons, was to safeguard the unquestioned position
of the Father who had not appeared in this world, and the
value of Christ's work, the value of revelation and of the
ransoming of mankind. History was to hold fast to this lesson.

Irenaeus, the holy bishop and martyr of Lyons, who died
about the year 202, is of exceptional importance. He also
fought the Gnostics, principally the one called Marcion, whose
lack of constraint in his attitude to the New Testament, especially St Luke's Gospel, is well known. Since matter and generation are utterly evil, it was not possible that Jesus should be
born of a woman, so Marcion arbitrarily suppressed the flower
of St Luke's writings, the stories of the annunciation and
childhood.

Irenaeus therefore set out to show that God is truly the
origin of matter, but humanity, created in a somewhat rudi-
mentary spiritual condition, needed to be educated by God and
raised from imperfection to a more perfect state. Excellent
educator that he is, God was leading man towards perfection.
But the sin of Adam and Eve interfered at this point. When
they were not yet capable of much discernment, at the dawn
of the human race, they were cheated by the devil, a much
greater sinner than they. God's genius—and his power—lay in
overcoming the devil's plots and man's very real fall, by carrying on with the education of the race. The Word was the
means for this. In this striking view of God's plans Adam's
sin and humanity's restoration were given an understandable
and coherent explanation. The Word, in the Old Testament
theophanies and then in his Incarnation, was appointed to be
humanity's Saviour.

Henceforward man's life and his spiritual progress consist
in sharing in God's life which has been given back to him in
Jesus Christ. The life of the Trinity itself is the way which
leads to divine intimacy. To explain this St Irenaeus is fond of
referring to the baptismal creed. Here he recalls the rule of
faith :

> Error has strangely departed from the truth about the three
> principal articles of our baptism. In fact they [the Gnostics]

either despise the Father, or refuse acceptance to the Son by rejecting the plan of his Incarnation, or they refuse to admit the Holy Spirit, that is they despise prophecy. We must beware of all these unbelievers and shun their society, if we really want to be pleasing to God, and reach salvation through him. (*Demonstration*, 100.)

Here, then, is the way of salvation:

The Father bears at once both Creation and his Word, and the Word borne by the Father gives the Spirit to all, according to the Father's will. To some in a manner suited to created beings, works of God; to others in a manner suited to children of God by adoption. In this way is made known one sole God, the Father who is above all things, and present to all things and in all things. Above all things is the Father, who is the head of Christ; the Word in his turn is present to all things, and he is the head of the Church; in all of us is the Spirit, and he is the living water which the Lord gives to those who truly believe in him and love him (*Against Heresy* 5. 18. 2).

Still more precisely does Irenaeus describe the rôle of the three Persons in the deification of Christians: the Father sends the Son, the Son becomes man so that we may become "Gods", but it is the Holy Spirit who brings us the pledge of it and presents us to the Father:

When we are born again by the baptism which is given to us in the name of these three Persons, we are enriched in this second birth with the good things which are in God the Father, by means of his Son, through the Holy Spirit. For those who are taken from the water receive the Spirit of God who presents them to the Word, that is to the Son; and the Son takes them and offers them to his Father, and the Father makes them partakers of incorruption. Thus, without the Spirit we cannot see the Word of God; and without the Son none can come to the Father, since knowledge of the Father is the Son, and knowledge of the Son is won by means of the Holy Spirit; but it is the Son who, by right of office, distributes the Spirit according to the Father's good pleasure, to those whom the Father wills, and as the Father wills. (*Demonstration*, 7.)

Such was the teaching given to Christians of the second century. Since the Son and the Holy Spirit possessed the power to deify, for this reason they must be God. This argument shut the heretics' mouths, and Christians could grow, through this living faith, in the three Persons, the sources of life.

THE FAITH OF THE APOSTLES' CREED

In the same living way was born the "I believe" which we use in our daily prayer and on the great occasions of our lives. Do we realize this when the godfather and godmother repeat it in the name of their godchild? When young people, just confirmed, repeat it in the power of the Spirit? And when our children repeat it on the day on which they bind themselves in person to the faith of their Baptism: do we, on these occasions, consider all that it represented in the first centuries of the Church?

I believe in God the Father,
I believe in the Son, the Saviour,
I believe in the Holy Spirit.

These formulas, nearly twenty centuries old, are still the seal of what we undertake in all the Christian sacraments, since the cleric also pronounces it on the day of his priestly ordination that is to make him the servant of the Word and teacher of the faith among the faithful; and since the dying man repeats with his last breath the changeless faith of twenty centuries and, we hope, of his whole life.

Christ had said: "You, therefore, must go out, making disciples of all nations, and baptizing them in the name of the Father and of the Son, and of the Holy Ghost" (Matt. 28. 19). So, after Pentecost, the apostles went, taught and baptized. The faith grew in their hearts, and the Church itself grew unceasingly (Acts 2. 41 and 47). But the need was for convinced Christians. In these first centuries, the acceptance of a new candidate as a member of the Church presupposed a voluntary decision on his part and a firm faith which it would be good to find nowadays in our Christians, and among adults who are preparing for baptism. The preliminary condition for admission to baptism was a knowledge of the mysteries of salvation, which were summed up in that of the Blessed Trinity. From the beginning it had been felt that Christ's command "Go . . . teach . . ." was a formal one, but that the regenerative waters of baptism could only be bestowed on believers. Also, in order to ensure the intellectual and spiritual preparation of the candidates, a number of professions of faith were composed which the catechumens[7] had to accept, and to profess on the day of their baptism. From the fourth century the profession of faith during Easter vigil was the final form of a custom originally rather simpler but basically identical with its later developments. In this way was the Lord's command fulfilled.

On the day of Pentecost St Peter had declared that baptism must be given in the name of Jesus Christ, that is, on his word and authority (read Acts 2. 38; 10. 48; 22. 16; and 1 Peter 3. 18–22).

St Paul also proclaimed the profession of faith in Christ as the indispensable condition of salvation (read Rom. 10. 9; 1 Cor. 8. 6; 12. 3–11; see also 1 John 4. 2–3). And the deacon Philip, according to some manuscripts, demanded the same attitude of mind from the Queen of Ethiopia's servant, whom he had just been catechising (Acts 8. 37).

In this way a course of action was laid down. It was now no longer possible to confer baptism without first hearing from the candidate's mouth the Christian profession of faith. Examples of this course abound in the second century, whether it be a question of the instruction given or of the rite itself.

Instruction in preparation for Baptism

The *Didache*, or the doctrine of the Lord taught to the nations by the twelve apostles,[8] devotes six chapters to tracing the path that the Christian must follow in order to be a disciple of the Lord. In Chapter 7 it says: "In the matter of baptism, baptize thus: after teaching all the foregoing, baptize in the

---

[7] A catechumen: one who listens to the teaching of Christ and practises it so as to become worthy of the grace of baptism.

[8] This document certainly dates from the middle of the second century. It was not written by the apostles, but endeavoured to teach their doctrine.

name of the Father, the Son and the Holy Spirit, in running water."

As we have seen, St Irenaeus of Lyons gave vigorous and clear instruction to the faithful in his charge.

Tertullian, about the year 200, bears witness for the Church in Africa of the same doctrine and the same practice:

> The law about baptism and the prescribed formula has been established thus: "Go, make disciples of all nations, and baptize them in the name of the Father and of the Son and of the Holy Ghost." To this law must be added the following decision: no one can enter into the kingdom of heaven unless he is born again of water and the Holy Spirit and this lays on faith the necessity of baptism. From which it follows that all who believe are to be baptized. (*Treatise on Baptism*, 13.)

The rite of baptism in the early Church

St Irenaeus' wonderful passage on the meaning of baptism, which is referred to above, does not describe the rite of baptism. But the *Didache* does. After giving the basic instruction it says: "Baptize in the name of the Father, the Son and the Holy Spirit, in running water. If you have no running water (that is, a stream or river), baptize in some other water, if you cannot do it in cold water, then use hot water. If you have neither, then pour water three times over the head in the name of the Father, of the Son and of the Holy Spirit" (Chapter 7).

Tertullian tells us nothing about the rite itself except in his writings against the heretic Praxeas, where he speaks of a triple confession of faith in the three Persons.

It is chiefly from the third and fourth centuries that we find documents containing descriptions of the rite of baptism. We shall go beyond the period we are studying in order to read the ritual which was certainly that of Rome in the third century, and was similar to that of the Church of Milan in the fourth.

The Apostolic Tradition, by St Hippolytus of Rome, is a most precious document on the customs of the third century. At that time, baptism was scarcely ever given except to adults, after a long initiation into the mysteries of the faith. These were summarized in a profession of faith, or "creed". At the moment of the administration of the first Christian sacrament, the recitation of the creed bore witness to the catechumen's personal act of adherence to God, the Three-in-One. But we must not imagine a furtive little rite such as we too often see today, with a thin trickle of water over the forehead. The rite was seldom reduced to a single pouring of water over the head. Usually people were baptized in rivers or in the already existing baptisteries which the art of the fourth and fifth centuries brought to perfection and of which magnificent remains are to be found in North Africa, Italy and France.[9] The candidate for baptism, then, went down into the river or into the baptismal pool. He was questioned on the principal articles of the faith, on the faith he must have in the Trinity. At each affirmative response he was immersed. Here is the text of the *Tradition of Hippolytus*:

> Let him [the catechumen] go down into the water and let him who baptizes lay his hand on his head, saying, "Do you believe in God the Father Almighty?" And let him who is being baptized reply, "I believe". Then let him be baptized once, keeping the hand still on his head. Then let him say, "Do you believe in Jesus Christ, the Son of God, who was born through the Holy Spirit of the Virgin Mary, died and was buried, and rose alive from the dead on the third day, has gone up to heaven, is seated at the right hand of the Father, and will come to judge the living and the dead?" And when he has said "I believe", let him baptize him again.
>
> Let him say again, "Do you believe in the Holy Spirit, in holy Church and in the resurrection of the body?" Let him who is being baptized say, "I believe". And so let him be baptized a third time.

In the following century St Ambrose of Milan in his explanation of the "sacraments" or sacred rites of the Church, gives evidence of an identical ritual.

[9] For example, the baptistery of St John Lateran in Rome, or that at Fréjus in France.

The present-day Creed

The "I believe" that we use now took its origin from that ancient tradition of the Church, the baptismal profession of faith. Basically nothing has changed except that it has perhaps lost the spiritual meaning that we no longer know how to discover in its text. It seems to us only a poor relation compared to the splendour of the other liturgical rites of the Church. And perhaps we devalue it by substituting for it our own prayers which contain only our own story, our own unsupported faith, our own enfeebled love, instead of finding in it twenty centuries of living faith.

For it is this which requires emphasis, the creed of our faith, the creed of the great days of our life, contains a whole history, mingled both with the rites of baptism and with the struggles against the spread of the early heresies.

The creed which we usually recite is called the "agreed text". It has been so since the sixth century, but it has only been used in the western liturgy since the Carolingian period (ninth century). Yet there was another before this one, a young, very humble brother, but in its humility and brevity most rich in its teaching. It was discovered less than forty years ago. All it does is soberly to declare faith in the Trinity. "I believe in the Father almighty, and in Jesus Christ our Saviour, and in the holy Spirit the Paraclete, in the holy Church and for the remission of sins" (sometimes also: "for the resurrection of the body").

We can guess the reason for this sobriety. During the first two centuries Trinitarian errors were not yet fully developed, but they were weighty, so a very simple formula of faith was enough. But gradually heresies grew up. They were aimed both at the dogma of the Trinity and at the person of Christ. They established the need to make the professions of faith more explicit. People must believe not only in the Trinity and in Christ but in the *work* of the Trinity and in the *different manifestations* of Christ. The Trinitarian formula originated in Christ's command (Matt. 28. 19); the Christological formula took shape from that laid down by St Paul (Rom. 10. 9; see

Acts 8. 37): it is necessary to believe in Jesus the Saviour.[10]

Towards the year 200 the two formulas, already amplified, were united to form the creed called the "Roman Creed" which is slightly shorter than ours. This creed was, and ours remains, the touchstone of Christian faith: the faith of the apostles is summed up in it.

One last remark must round off these reflections about our creed. Abbé Pierre Nautin has shown us how we ought to understand the third question in the rite of baptism. The writings of the Fathers of the Church of the first centuries tell us quite frequently that the Church is holy because the Holy Spirit lives in her, and that the Holy Spirit is given *for* the remission of sins, and lastly, *for* the resurrection of the body. It will have been noticed that this was the meaning of the profession of faith in the Holy Spirit in our ancient creed. The third question at baptism, then, should be as follows: "Do you believe in the Holy Ghost, in holy Church for the resurrection of the body?" So the end of our creed would make better sense if we read it: "I believe in the Holy Ghost, in the holy Catholic Church, the communion of saints, for the remission of sins, the resurrection of the body and life everlasting."

CHRISTIAN PRAYER

Professions of faith are not the only documents we can consult in order to learn about Christian life in the second century. Personal daily prayer, that of the Christian assembly, provides us with a number of clues. The prayer of the first Christians was very much a continuation of that of St Paul and St John, with this one difference: in the first century people did not pray to the Trinity, or to the Holy Spirit; only the Father and Christ were addressed. From the second century, people began to alter their spiritual bearings; praise was given to the whole Trinity. We shall take a few of these first Christian prayers,

[10] This was the origin of the acrostic $IX\Theta Y\Sigma$, whose five letters in Greek are the initials of "Jesus Christ, Son of God, Saviour", but which together make the word for "fish". So the fish became a symbol of Jesus Christ, Son of God, our Saviour.

once more anticipating the third century so as to provide a richer anthology.

The eucharistic doxologies

These are to be found inserted in the Mass, already a living thing as we find it in the works of St Justin. In the prayer which we now call the Preface and that the Greeks referred to as the "anaphora" (a "sending up" or thanksgiving), we find an ending just like our own. *The Apostolic Tradition* of Hippolytus of Rome serves again as our source. The anaphora of Hippolytus begins, like our Preface, with a dialogue. It goes on with praises of God, includes the consecration and the memorial prayer that recalls the great events in the life of Christ (*Unde et memores*), and finishes like this: "We praise you (Father) and we glorify you through your Son Jesus Christ, through whom honour and glory are yours, to the Father and the Son, with the Holy Spirit, in your holy Church, now and in the ages to come. Amen."

Then as now, the sacrifice of the Mass was offered to God the Father through Jesus Christ. But it is also noticeable in this text that praise is directed to the Son and the Holy Spirit together with the Father. In the rites of blessing used at this period, this same form is constantly maintained.

Non-eucharistic doxologies

St Paul was in the habit of writing prayers that sprang spontaneously from his pen, short forms in which he poured out his soul to the Father and to Christ. After the second century two sorts of doxology, both still familiar to us, formed an integral part of Christian prayer. The form most commonly used supplicates or gives praise to the Father *through* the Son *in union with* the Holy Spirit. That was the wish of St Paul for the Corinthians as he expressed it in the conclusion of his second letter to them. It is thus that we still pray in the collects of the Mass: *Per Dominum nostrum Jesum Christum . . . in unitate Spiritus Sancti . . .* ("Through our Lord Jesus Christ . . . in the unity of the Holy Spirit . . ."). But another form, a shorter one, was already part of the Christian heritage. Today it closes the singing of psalms or the decades of the rosary, to give praise, on an equal footing, to Father, Son and Holy Spirit: it is our *Gloria Patri, et Filio, et Spiritui Sancto* ("Glory be to the Father and to the Son and to the Holy Ghost"). First used at the beginning of the second century, and well known to St Irenaeus, it became in the fourth century a most useful weapon against the Arian heresy. St Basil demonstrated victoriously to those who denied the divinity of the Spirit that their error contradicted the traditional faith of the Church, which is not afraid to honour the Spirit equally with the other two Persons. And St Ambrose, besieged by the Arians in his basilica at Milan, found in the *Gloria Patri* spiritual support for his faithful Christians: he used this doxology to make a refrain which he inserted between the verses of the psalms, and the crowd took up the response with fervour, glorifying God and so protesting against that tenacious heresy which denied the equality of the three Persons.

Hymns

Hymns are the breaking out of religious feeling in rhythmic form. Jews and pagans had written them. The first Christians did not despise this way of praying. Already in St Paul we heard the first hymns to Christ. And the younger Pliny, a pagan, reported to the Emperor Trajan: "The Christians sing hymns to Christ, as to a God." In this respect also the second century is a Trinitarian one.

The oldest known hymn to the Trinity is certainly the one called "Joyful Light", which was used in the East as a Vesper hymn. The three Persons are praised with perfect equality: "Joyful Light of the holy glory of the immortal Father; heavenly, holy and blessed, Jesus Christ. Now at the hour of sunset, seeing the evening light, we sing hymns to the Father, the Son, and the Holy Spirit of God. You are worthy to be praised at all times by strong voices, Son of God, you who give life. It is for this that the world gives you glory."

Another hymn, better known to us, is the *Gloria in excelsis* of the Mass. Some manuscripts give it without mention of the Holy Spirit, but others preserve the text that we still sing in our liturgical assembly.

Are we such a long way from that time of faith and prayer? Today, as in the Africa of Tertullian's time, the Christian makes the sign of the cross, the sign of redemption. But with it he uses a Trinitarian form of words. Our *Gloria Patri* has not changed either, nor the *Gloria in excelsis* of the Mass. The conclusion of all our solemn prayers reminds us of the mystery of how Christ ransoms us and our deification in the Holy Spirit, to the glory of God the Father. Our Canon, the unchanging part of the Mass, includes the wonderful *Per ipsum*, which proclaims that through Christ, in the Spirit, all things are given back to the Father. And before Communion we, with the priest, can say the three prayers of petition, the second of which is Trinitarian. Finally each year we celebrate the Trinity in that solemnity of which a writer of the twelfth century, Rupert de Tuy, could write: "After we have celebrated the coming of the Holy Spirit, on the following Sunday we sing the glory of the blessed Trinity. For, immediately after the descent of the divine Spirit began the preaching of, and belief in, the Father, the Son, and the Holy Spirit; and in baptism, faith and confession were made in their name."

To bring certain solemn rites to a close, and to give thanks to God, Three-in-One, the Church thunders the triumphant *Te Deum*. Age follows age, the faith does not change, but sometimes it slumbers. May this Christian prayer, whose roots go down to the very springs of the faith, serve to awaken it.

CHAPTER VI

THE TRINITY IN PERIL IN
THE THIRD CENTURY

THE TRINITY, SYMBOL OR REALITY?

Was it enough that the Christian teachers of the second century had victoriously affirmed their faith and that of the Church in the three divine Persons, and had anchored it in the souls of the faithful? To suppose so would be to forget the exacting quality of the human mind. Man cannot merely *believe*: he demands also to *know*. But in the second century their faith was deeper than they knew; they lived their faith more than they explained it. It is therefore not surprising if we encounter explanations of the Trinity which could not be accepted by those whose business it was to supervise the teaching of the true meaning of the faith.[1]

---

[1] It should not be supposed that a heretic is at first a person of ill-will. He is a seeker and a thinker, but one who seeks and thinks *alone*, that is, he allows himself to be guided by human reasoning instead of seeking light in the faith of the Church, faith and light that are not refused by God when a man is faithful to the Holy Spirit living in the Church. The rule of faith is *Tradition* which is the living organ in which it is to be found and on the foundation of which further reflection is possible. St Paul's advice to Timothy (2 Tim. 4. 3–5) should be borne in mind together with the golden rule laid down by St Vincent of Lérins: "Teach what you have learnt in order not to invent, but explain things in a new way." See Volume 136 in this series.

In the history of theology the chief heresy of the third century is called Modalism and Monarchianism or Sabellianism. What do these names mean?

The "Modalists" or "Monarchians" in their itch to explain everything were guided by the desire to maintain at any cost the divine unity or "monarchy". At the same time, because they wanted to go about their task like good theologians, they were concerned to safeguard the divinity of Jesus Christ. But they only achieved this by declaring that there is no distinction of persons between the Father and the Son, nor between them and the Holy Spirit. There is but one God, who is called Father in the Old Testament. This Father-God became incarnate in the Virgin Mary, he was born of her, and by his birth in time became his own son, he who is called "the Son of God". So it was the Father-God, become his own son, who suffered on the cross. The opponents of the error gave to this particular "monarchian" error the name of "Patripassianism", meaning the heresy that it was the Father-God who suffered. Finally it was he also who rose again. Often they found it enough to talk of the Father and the Son; the Holy Spirit was passed over in silence.

Since, they said, the Father had manifested himself as Son, that is under another *mode*, this error was also denounced under the name of "Modalism". Their conclusion was that the Word has no existence of his own. Tertullian said to Praxeas: "to you the Word is what you will, a *flatus vocis*, a syllable."

The two principal propagators of this heresy were Praxeas, against whom Tertullian measured himself, and Noëtus, whose adversary was Hippolytus of Rome. But soon another, Sabellius, came to complete the heresy.

He worked to perfect this unitarian system. He imagined one God, a God who was one unique person, or *prosopon* (a Greek word meaning "person"), and who played a number of different parts in history. The one person or divine *prosopon* manifested himself in diverse modes (so the idea is still "modalist"): as law-giver in the Old Testament—that is the Father; as redeemer in Jesus—that is the Son; as sanctifier in the Church —that is the Holy Spirit. By his three-faceted but unique *prosopon* Sabellius avoided Patripassianism, he no longer put the Father on the cross. But by dint of explaining it he destroyed the divine Trinity. Obviously, it had become necessary to add knowledge to faith if the faith itself was not to be lost.

TERTULLIAN AGAINST PRAXEAS

Tertullian, the great African teacher of the third century, was born about the years 150–60. Converted in 195, he unfortunately turned Montanist[2] in 206, and died about 240–50. It was between 213 and 218 that he met Praxeas whom he reproached with having performed a doubly diabolic work: by not mentioning the Holy Spirit he deprived the Church of all prophetic power; secondly, he had crucified the Father.

Unity and Trinity

The great problem facing Tertullian was that of giving a proper account of these two aspects of God. It was necessary to admit the reality of the Trinity, the real existence in him of three Persons, the divine unity notwithstanding. This was his profession of faith: he believed in the divine "monarchy" (unity) just as much as Praxeas did; in opposition to him he held that there are three Persons in God. This is how he explained it:

God eternally contains in himself a "reason" (*ratio*), in which there is a "word" (*sermo*) which is his thought and his wisdom. When God wished to create, his Word, who is his Son, was uttered. When God wished to redeem, the Word entered into the Virgin and, born of her, was called Jesus Christ. But, before the coming of the Son, God possessed his own eternal mystery. We must avoid, says Tertullian, the novelties of

[2] Montanism was the heresy of Montanus who said that the only people who should have authority to teach in the Church were those who were truly spiritual, that is, guided by the Holy Spirit. This was the first attempt to oppose the established hierarchy of the Church. Montanus thought that the Church was without doctrinal authority when she ceased to be "spiritual". He set himself up as the chosen organ through which the Holy Spirit spoke, but every "Montanist" had some share in these prerogatives. See Volume 136 in this series.

Praxeas. We must understand the living God in this way: there is but one God, that is, one unique divine substance. Nevertheless, in the heart of this unity is to be found a mystery (one which we might be tempted to call "domestic"), which constitutes a unity in Trinity: Father, Son and Holy Spirit. Not that these three are three in essence[3] (*status*), but they are three according to the degree or rank (*gradus*) in which we think of them (that is, they are arranged in a hierarchy). They are not three in substance but three in their particular characters (*forma*); not three in their power which remains one, but three in their individual relationship (*species*). So we affirm one sole God, of one unique substance, one unique essence and one unique power, but this one God is three in rank, in particular character, and in the different aspects which are manifested in him.

Degrees in God

But we require a more developed analysis of the different ranks which allow us to find "number" in God, and an examination of the order of the appearance of Father, Son and Spirit. Here, Tertullian makes use of what he, an African, has noticed. His timid sketch of the Word to be found in the divine reason is discarded. The theologian looks about him, and the land of Africa offers itself quite naturally as a symbol of God. It helps him to explain the "degrees" in which the three Persons are arranged. He abandons the "domestic" mystery of God. He thinks of him now, in the manner of St Irenaeus, as God who is the source of life for us. The first Person is the Father, the source of all things; the second is the Son, agent of grace; the third is the Spirit who comes to give life to our souls.

The images are many, they sing, they live. First there is that of the delicious *fruit*. It is the symbol of the Holy Spirit; we pick it off the *branch* (an image of the Son); but the branch itself would be nothing without the *root* which feeds it—an image of the Father, the origin of all life. The root is the symbol of the Father, the branch of the Son, and the fruit, the

---

[3] The essence, or nature of a thing, is that which constitutes it. It is the practical equivalent of the words substance and nature.

object of desire, for whose sake the root and the branch are lovingly tended, is the symbol of the Holy Spirit who is given to us. The Holy Spirit comes from the Father through the Son.

Here, next, comes the very African idea of the spring, the river and the irrigation canal. When we remember what the soil of Tunis is like, dried up by the heat of the sun, sterile and arid for lack of water, Tertullian's image creates a vivid picture, like that of the Psalmist's verse: "O God, thou art my God; how eager my quest for thee, body athirst and soul longing for thee, like some parched wilderness, where stream is none! (62. 2).

Water is a blessing in dry countries. But neither the spring nor the river are any use unless the irrigation canals are there to carry the life-giving water and spread it over the scorched earth: "Water, you are life", said Saint-Exupéry. The image of the Father, then, is the spring; the Son is the river that flows from the paternal source; but the irrigation canals are the wonderful symbol of the Spirit poured out upon souls.

The last image is also an African one. Let us forget the evils of the long summer heats. In the spring and autumn the sun is the life-bringing god, awakening nature from its winter sleep, from its death in the summer dog days. Water has come, but without the sun it would be more harmful than useful. Here, the sun is the Father. The beam which he sends forth is the Son. But the beam which the sun never ceases to send out, only becomes a bringer of life to us when its delicate point touches and warms us. This point is the symbol of the Spirit, bearer of heat and life.

Such was the refutation that Tertullian used against the heresy of Praxeas. The Trinity does not destroy the divine unity, he said, rather it makes it reasonable. The Trinity is the mystery of the one God. Though he is far from merely being manifested in three different modes, he does consist of a kind of "family arrangement" which shows him to be perfectly organized in himself. It may seem that these explanations are not explicit enough, that they lack strength to fathom the mystery. That is true, but the time had not yet come to search closely, as St Augustine was to do, into the depths of God's mystery. Can we regret that, instead, he speaks to us of God in images that live and vibrate? To reproach him with this would be to accuse St Paul and St John as well, for they themselves thought of the Holy Spirit as the messenger of the Father and the Son, sent to clothe us with divine life.

He may be forgiven the lines he wrote to Hermogenes, in which he seemed to deny the eternity of the Son. At that time (about 200) his thought was less sure. He did not dare to call God, Father, nor to say that there was a Son before the "Word" had come to redeem man's sin. If "the Son" is the redeemer, then until there is sin to be destroyed there is no redeemer and, therefore, no Son. Once the "Word" had been born of the Virgin, once the Son was there, then God could be called Father. Certainly this text is much less precise than the refutation of Praxeas. But even here Tertullian does not deny that there is an eternal "Word"; only he would not call him "Son", as Scripture does, until he had appeared among men. God could be called "Father" only from that time onwards.

From the work of the great theologian from Carthage we should remember, then, the wonderful *distinction* he describes in God: the unity of nature and the distinction of persons, and the order of their advent in deified man: the Spirit comes from the Father through the Son. Hence he is God, and it is God's life that he brings us. Tertullian's name is at the head of the list of great theologians who have made it possible by their formulas to speak of God, one and three, without confusion: "There are three Persons in God but one unique substance." But he is also a man of the spirit, who knows that life, for man, is the possession of God's life through the Spirit.

From the pen of the great Tertullian had flowed rich and abundant images, human thought had made a noble effort. But the absolute equality of the divine Persons had still to be proclaimed. To establish this was to be the difficult task of the fourth century.

CHAPTER VII

THE STRUGGLE AGAINST

ARIANISM

THE ARIANS AND THE PNEUMATOMACHIANS

Discussions on vocabulary

About the year 265 Denis, Bishop of Alexandria, anxious to establish carefully the distinction between the divine Persons, gave in his theology an inferior rank to the Son and the Holy Spirit. At least, Denis expressed himself in such a way that it would be possible later to misunderstand his thought. The difficulty lay in formulating in precise language the doctrine of God, Three-in-One. There were some old formulas in existence but they had become outmoded in the previous century. They had made it possible to talk about God and his creative Word, but would they still serve that purpose? That was the problem to be considered.

Since the second century it had been said that God was "unbegotten", meaning that he derived from no other being, that he was without origin. And it could equally be said of this "unbegotten" God that he was "not-made", that he did not become, in other words that he was not created. (In Greek this is expressed by two words, differing only in a single letter: ἀγέννητος, unbegotten; ἀγένητος, uncreated.) But besides God, there is his creation. Obviously this was not "unbegotten" or "uncreated". All the same, could it be called "begotten"?

No, because to be "begotten" supposes sonship. So it is clear that creation was not "begotten"; it was made (γενητος). But the question recurred when applied to the Word of God. It was customary to say that the Word, God's Son, had been begotten by him. But if he is begotten we cannot at the same time think of him as "unbegotten" (ἀγέννητος). It is possible, however, to call him uncreated (ἀγένητος), as Pope Denis proclaimed. So the Word of God is uncreated and begotten (γεννητός). Could he be described as "made", "become", "created" (γενητος)? Denis had forbidden it and, in fact, Christian teachers rejected the idea. At the beginning of the third century Origen judged this expression to be unsuitable in speaking of the Son of God. But another teacher arose who was less particular.

Arius and his doctrine

Arius (256–336) was a priest of Alexandria, ordained about 310. Trained by the Modalist and Monarchian teachers of Antioch, the oneness of God was precious to him above all else. But the influence of Alexandria made itself felt equally; there, people distinguished the divine Persons to the point of separating them, and also placed the Son and the Holy Spirit in a position inferior to that of the Father. It must be added that Arius was soaked in neo-platonist philosophy. The peculiarity of this philosophy consisted in placing above all beings one sole God, called the *One,* who nevertheless assumed a lower rank as *Intelligence,* and the *Soul of the world,* two intermediaries between One-God and the world. Out of these different elements Arius constructed his trinitarian system.

God is one. His essential quality is to be unbegotten; he alone is eternal and without origin. But God could not communicate his nature to anyone at all. Such a communication would require him to be divisible, that is, composite, capable of change. God, simple, pure spirit, is none of these things. What is the result? That every thing that comes from God is necessarily begotten or, better, created. This is precisely the position of the Word of God. Certainly he is described as begotten, but it is clear that everything begotten of God is also necessarily created, that is, made by him. In any case, whether the Word is referred to as begotten or created, it all comes to the same thing: since the essential property of God is to be unbegotten, he cannot be God. To be begotten is thus the equivalent of being created. So the Word is neither God nor eternal. That is why God the Father is alone eternal, alone immutable, while the Word, made by him, is not. All the same, Arius is careful not to place him on an equal footing with other creatures. The Word was made before them, before time and space existed, and time and space only began from the moment when there were measurable creatures, that is, extended in space and mobile. Hence the Word existed before all ages, he was God's instrument in creation. Apt use of the Bible supplied Arius with a good argument. The book of Proverbs (8. 22), which Arius read in Greek, said that God "made" Wisdom before creation began. But Wisdom is the Word. And the Gospel in its turn teaches that Jesus, the Son of God, declared: "The Father is greater than I" ("My Father has greater power than I" in the Knox version—John 14. 28). So the Word of God really is his Son; it can even be admitted that he is "God coming from God", "Light coming from the Light". But it is clear that this is so only in a degraded, inferior sense. The Word of God could not be God equally with the unbegotten Father.

A BISHOP DEFENDS THE FAITH: ST ALEXANDER OF ALEXANDRIA

The Bishop of Alexandria was called Alexander; he died in 328. In 320 he condemned Arius. As a theologian he had not the breadth of knowledge of his successor St Athanasius (who accompanied the bishop to Alexandria, and who in 325 was only a deacon); he was nevertheless a man of faith, learned in the Scriptures, able to reflect deeply on them. Above all he was a saint, and a man of that kind always has a sense of the meaning of the faith. So we find him opposing Arius with the text from Hebrews 1. 3, where the Son is called "the radiance of his Father's splendour, and the full expression of his being". He found in this an indication of the Son's divinity. Besides, said he, can anyone imagine that the Father was, at one time, without Word and without Wisdom, in other words does anyone dare to say that God is a spirit who does not think? Impossible. Hence there is eternally in God an interior "Word" who is his Son, as eternal and immutable as the Father whose thought he is. He is the uncreated Word, begotten none the less by the eternal intelligence of the Father.

THE COUNCIL OF NICEA

In the fourth Christian century the Emperors meddled in Church affairs with authority. Her peace depended on the good order of the state. Governing all things as the representative of God on earth that he was held to be, the Emperor Constantine called a council to settle an affair that might disturb the peace of the state, and 318 bishops gathered at Nicea, a town of Anatolia in Asia Minor. They came both from the East and West. The large number of bishops present, whom Pope Sylvester encouraged by sending his own representatives, caused the council to be known as "ecumenical", that is, representing all the earth. Nicea was the first council to be called ecumenical. The work of the 318 bishops, the "Fathers" (of the faith), at the council is summed up in the Creed they composed. This was a first attempt which was to be perfected at the end of the century, after the council of Constantinople, in 381. It is this second text that we sing during Mass as our "Credo", known as that of Nicea-Constantinople. This is the teaching we find in it:

The Son is begotten, only Son of one substance with the Father. It is precisely stated that he was not made or created. Therefore he does not belong to the order of creatures, even as their head. He is proclaimed "true God coming from true God", but this phrase is given greater precision by an important word: the Son is "consubstantial" with the Father: *consubstantialem Patri*, as we sing the Creed.

To be exact, this term means "of the same essence"; and such precision was important in order to leave no loopholes for the heresy of Arius. To say that the Son was "true God coming from true God" was no longer enough. In the neo-platonist philosophy adopted by Arius, a diminished God was still truly God. The inferior beings who come forth directly from God are still divine although subordinate. So Arius found no difficulty in calling the Son "true God" and, at the same time, refusing him divinity in the sense that the Father possessed it. A divine being like the Word, the first to come forth from God, is God, yet without being unbegotten, which is the prerogative of the one God alone. Already written in the Creed was the expression "Light coming from the Light". This had been enough for Tertullian to refute the error of Praxeas; it was useless to silence Arius. Finally, it was necessary to define with precision the language of Scripture, which resembled Arius' language too closely. Psalm 81 proclaimed: "Gods you are, I have said it", and St Paul himself called Christians "sons of God". Hence a technical word was needed. When, before its existence, the Patriarch Denis of Alexandria seemed to show a leaning towards the Arian heresy, the Greek term *homo-ousios* (consubstantial) had already been suggested. It now recurs. Since Arius declared the Son to be "in all things unlike the Father", in opposition to him the council affirmed that the Word-Son is, on the contrary, of the same substance as the Father, identical with him in all things. Hence the Father and Son are equal. This was what they said, this and no more. They did not yet say that the nature of Father and Son is *one*. It was only later that, thanks to the Latins and in particular to the great Hilary of Poitiers, language and thought reached such a degree of precision. "Consubstantial" (*homoousios*) now expressed the unity of the divine nature. Father and Son together have one nature. For the time being, heresy had been strangled, and faith in the divinity of the Son could continue to be effective in the lives of Christians.

Against Nicea

The adherents of Nicea, like the council itself, were unable to settle all subsequent difficulties. Crypto-Arians took advantage of certain confusions of terminology to obtain the rejection, or at least the watering down, of the established dogma.

Some strict Arians were called "Anomoeans", because they said that the Word is unlike the Father, since he is created by him. Eunomius was the leader of this party. Others attempted reconciliation, but not to the extent of accepting the "homoousios" of Nicea. They wanted, by changing one letter of the word, to say that the Word is "like in substance" (*homoiousios*) to the Father. They were called Homoians. Basil of Ancyra was behind this "conservative" plan. Finally a third party was formed under Acacius, the aged Bishop of Caesarea. This was the "Homoean" party, because they considered that it was enough to say that the Word is "like" (*homoios*) the Father. But there was a good deal of knavery mixed up in all this. What they all wanted was to undermine the faith established by the 318 Fathers of Nicea, which Athanasius was already bravely defending. His courage earned him a long exile by the Emperor. On his side, St Hilary (also exiled, but in the East) opposed all these parties. His return to Gaul was implored, for Arianism was spreading, and its leaders enjoyed the support of the Emperors they had managed to deceive. This was so evident that in Jerusalem St Jerome, watching all these struggles, exclaimed: "The whole world began to groan, and in its stupor realized that it had become Arian!"

THE HOLY SPIRIT IS BANISHED FROM THE TRINITY

Arianism filled all minds, but in spite of it the work done at Nicea was making its mark. Now a new difficulty arose. So far attention had been concentrated on the Son, whether to deny or affirm his divinity, but little had been said of the Holy Spirit. We have now come to about the year 360.

The heresy of the Pneumatomachians

Since nowhere does Scripture give to the Holy Spirit the name of God, or say that he is a creature, or declare him eternal, conclusions began to be drawn from this. Eustace of Sebaste declared: "For my part I would not dare to give to the Holy Spirit the name of God, nor," he added, "the name of creature." Others, less scrupulous, asserted: "Since it is written that all things were made by the Word, the word *all*

includes the Holy Spirit. Hence he is a creature." Besides, they
pointed out, if the Holy Spirit were God, if he came from the
Father as the Word did, then there would be two sons, and
hence two brothers in the Trinity. Such a hypothesis was obviously unacceptable, and so the Holy Spirit was given an
intermediate position between God and a creature. The Holy
Spirit must not be adored as God, nor receive "equal honour"
with the Father and the Son.

Since this error consisted in opposing the godhead of the
Holy Spirit, its adherents were known by the name of Pneu-
matomachians ("those who fight against the Spirit"). It was
also called the "Macedonian Heresy", from Macedonius,
Patriarch of Constantinople, who was supposed to profess it
(359).

The champions of Catholic orthodoxy

Here we encounter again the former deacon, Athanasius,
who some time before had succeeded St Alexander in the see
of Alexandria. At this time his genius was at its height. The
writings in which he describes the Arian heresy and the sittings
of the Council of Nicea (at which, it will be remembered, he
was present) give evidence of mature theological thought. He
was ready to oppose the new heresy. His letters to Serapion,
Bishop of Thmuis in Egypt, have preserved his teaching for
us, a doctrine whose richness astonishes and nourishes us to
this day.

Athanasius began by establishing that a knowledge of the
divinity of the Word is the primary element in an accurate
demonstration of the divinity of the Spirit. But there was no
easy way of proving that the Word is God save by beginning
with his power to deify. This, it will be remembered, was the
theological reasoning already propagated by St Irenaeus: "If
Christ can make us divine, then he cannot be a creature." But
the common belief, even among those who denied the divinity
of the Spirit, was that he, also, has the power to make us
divine. St Athanasius explains thus:

It is also by the Holy Spirit that we are all called sharers in
God. In fact Paul says: "Surely you know that your bodies are
the shrines of the Holy Spirit, who dwells in you. And he is

God's gift to you." If someone destroys the shrine of God, God will destroy him in his turn, for the shrine of God which you are, is Holy. Now if the Holy Spirit were a creature, we could have no share in God through him; we should be joined to a creature and strangers to the divine nature, since we would have no share in it. But now that we are called sharers in the Son, and sharers in God, it is apparent that the activity, and the seal, which is in us has not the nature of created things, but the nature of the Son who, by the Spirit which is in him, unites us to the Father. This is, in fact, what St John taught when he wrote: "This is our proof that we are dwelling in him (God) and he in us; he has given us a share in his own Spirit". But if, by sharing in the Spirit, we become sharers in the divine nature, a man would be senseless if he were to say that the Spirit belongs to created nature and not to that of God. In fact that is the reason why those in whom he dwells are deified. And if he can deify, there can be no doubt that his nature is that of God. (*First letter to Serapion*, 1. 24.)

Finally, a weighty argument from Scripture; certainly Scripture nowhere gives to the Holy Spirit the name of God, but it does better than that. First of all it teaches us his origin: the Holy Spirit does not come from nothing but from the Father and the Son (John 14. 15–26). Also Scripture numbers him, not in the order of creatures, but with the Father and Son (Rom. 8. 1–17; Matt. 28. 19). Hence he is God. The activity of the Spirit and the rank he holds in the divine realm, according to Athanasius, prove his divinity (*First Letter to Serapion*, 1. 14, 17, 22).

But Athanasius was no longer alone in this struggle for the faith. Other teachers were there to cast light on the matter. For all the importance of his rôle and the richness of his doctrine, there was still need for an expert in language. In fact there were three who brought this work to a successful conclusion. In history they are called the "three Cappadocians". They are St Basil of Caesarea, St Gregory of Nyssa, and the friend of both, St Gregory Nazianzen. The vigorous thought and precise wording of St Basil—the only one we can discuss here—were to bring about the final defeat of a very persistent error.

St Basil of Caesarea

He became the leader of Catholic orthodoxy between 370 and 379. It is to him that we owe the precision of the terms we have used ever since to refer to both the nature of the one God and the Trinity of Persons. It will be remembered that Tertullian had said: "one substance and three persons". But there did not yet exist in Greek a vocabulary equivalent to the Latin one.

Basil therefore declared that there is in God *one sole nature*, or essence that really exists: that is, the *ousia*, that Father, Son and Holy Spirit have in common. But in God faith distinguishes three "subjects". Why? Because the divine essence, although one, possesses characteristics which enable it to exist in three different ways. Therefore, if I consider the essence alone, I speak of one God: if I consider the essence with its "properties", I have Father, Son and Holy Spirit: to these three we will give the common name of *hypostasis*. We will therefore affirm that there is in God "one sole essence (or nature) and three hypostases (or persons)".

That was a bold stroke, for the Council of Nicea had affirmed the unity of the *ousia* (essence) or hypostasis, in God. But because, since Nicea, theologians had preferred to use hypostasis in the sense of "person", rather than "essence", Basil did not hesitate to change the meaning of the word from that which had been understood at Nicea. Now hypostasis means "subject". There are three in the Trinity, so there are three hypostases in God. Distinct in virtue of their properties, these hypostases are none the less identical, *consubstantial*, since there is in God but one essence which all three have in common. So there is "number" in the one God because of his characteristics, but at the same time there is the most absolute community of life in the one divine nature. Such was the immense labour of thought and of exact expression that Basil had successfully concluded in opposition to the heretic Eunomius. After this it was easy for him to claim for the Holy Spirit "equal honour" with that offered by creatures to Father and Son. Besides, he says in his treatise on the Holy Spirit, the Church knows this well, and has long been singing. "Glory be to the Father, and to the Son and to the Holy Ghost". The three are thus placed on an equal footing. It is this faith of St Basil which, as we shall see later, is preserved in the Creed at Mass.

One last comment: out of consideration for the scriptural sensibilities of his opponents, St Basil never says: "The Holy Spirit is God". But as we have seen he does better, for he exacts for him joint adoration with that given to the Father and the Son.

At the end of these discussions in which the stake was the content of the faith and the very meaning of the Christian life, an era of peace was to begin. "Language is the source of mis-understandings", so the vocabulary had become exact: there is one nature in God, common to the three persons. The three persons are not "modes" of one nature, but subjects distinct in virtue of their personal characteristics: one is not another, but one is equal to another, since the nature of the three is one. So it was possible after this to study the mystery of the Trinity more thoroughly, to examine it more profoundly, as St Augustine was to do in the next century. Through the intellectual work of the theologians people were able to live more closely the "family life" of the three persons. A council—or rather a profession of faith—was to stamp these formulas with the seal of the universal Church.

THE CREED OF THE COUNCIL OF CONSTANTINOPLE

The creed which we sing at Mass is called the creed of Nicea-Constantinople because one tradition attributes its final form to this second ecumenical council. It is not certain that this is really its source. It is already to be found, as we have it, in St Epiphanius. However that may be, we shall keep its name and briefly examine its content.

It can be guessed that its especial emphasis is on the divinity of the Holy Spirit, since all that was essential concerning the Son had been said at Nicea. In this connection we find only slight modifications, such as the removal of the final anathema which forbade the description of the Son as coming from an *ousia* or hypostasis different from that of the Father. Since now hypostasis meant "person" it could not be made the equivalent of *ousia* or essence. There are one or two amplifications on the birth and rôle of Christ; on his birth by the Holy Spirit (an important point) and of the Virgin Mary; on his passion under Pontius Pilate, and his place at the right hand of the Father.

At Nicea the Holy Spirit had been the subject of one affirmation only: "I believe in the Holy Spirit." In this new form he is described as possessing Lordship. In the Greek text he is not called "Lord", because since St Paul this title was reserved to Christ, but he is described as having a (divine) Lordship, that is, as having the nature of God. Secondly, he is described as "life-giver", an idea that the Greek Fathers are known to have been fond of. He is said to proceed, that is to come forth, from the Father. St John's theology had triumphed.[1] Finally St Basil's doctrine has left its mark here: the Holy Spirit is not called "consubstantial" with the Father and the Son, but something that has the same meaning: he must be given "equal honour", he must be adored and glorified together with them: *simul adoratur et conglorificatur.*

In this way, towards the end of the fourth century, these painful quarrels ended; this did not, however, result in the union of the various parties which had broken off from the Church. But God, who can draw good from evil, had stirred up a great effort of thought so that the Catholic faith might be clarified. It was clear now in what way people should think of the Trinity. The future lay open to the theologians. The eastern doctors had taken a great deal of trouble, and their treatises, which were second to none in dogmatic precision, continued to strengthen the piety of the faithful. Later on we shall follow the main lines of their theology in which they explain for us the mysterious life of God, and the divine procession of the Son and the Spirit. But the time of the West was to come. Being less engaged in the struggle with heresy it could turn to peaceful meditation on the mystery of God. We shall see St Augustine, strengthened by a firm grasp of the

[1] For the well-known expression, *ex Patre Filioque*, see Chapter VIII. It was not put into the Creed until the ninth century.

terms used to express the Catholic faith, composing the greatest treatise on God that has ever been written. In his fifteen books he penetrated, if I may dare to say so, to the very heart of the Trinity. It was to this masterpiece of faith and learning that St Thomas Aquinas, the prince of theologians, was to return in the thirteenth century, to bring it to the final perfection of intellectual precision. These are the labours which we must now examine, and through them we shall learn a little more of the truth about God. But we shall also learn from it a little more of what precisely is man created in his image, and again, what exactly it is man's duty to be, in this world where God has placed him.

PART III

BELIEVING, KNOWING, LIVING THE FAITH IN THE LIVING GOD

*I invoke thee, God of truth . . .
that I may know thee*
(St Augustine, *Soliloquies*)

The first Christian centuries were centuries of intense faith in the Trinity and in the second section of this book they have acted as our spiritual guides. But we must take another step forward in this third part and see how the dogma of the Trinity was expressed in terms of human reason in the Christian East which had been the setting of so many conflicts. We must see how it is expressed nowadays by eastern Catholics and by certain of our separated brethren. We must mark the limits of the gap that separates these last from both eastern and western Catholics, and follow the main outlines of the theology of these two divisions of Christendom.

It would be an over-simplification to imagine that the mystery of the ineffable God could be explained and presented in one way only. Through the centuries Christian thought has been too lively to be confined to a single line of development. On the contrary, history shows us that two different spirits, the Greek and the Latin, have expressed in two different ways the Trinitarian mystery. It is worth the theologian's while to examine them, for they contain riches. But we may also hope that when other civilizations come to be integrated into the Catholic Church, the cultural and philosophical wealth of these countries too may perhaps become a valuable instrument to help us to speak more worthily of the living God. Far from being a danger to the faith of the Church, every human culture, once it has been absorbed into Christianity and purified by it, becomes a new beacon to light up the mysteries of the faith. Apart from anything else, this is a considerable missionary problem. If India were to hear the word of Christ and be converted, it is possible that she would be hardly capable of considering the divine mystery in the ways traditional to the Christian East and West, full of living inspiration though they are. Young in the faith and proud of her own cultural heritage, she might give us instead a Hindu theology of the Trinity.

This problem which is always with us was obviously present from the beginning of Christianity. The temptation to go no further than the synagogue was not an empty phrase. But what would have happened if St Athanasius had not made use of Greek thought as well as Scripture, if he had not so vigorously proclaimed the *homoousios*, or if Basil had thought that questions of vocabulary did not matter? It is obviously impossible to guess. The faith would not have died, for the Church is in possession of Christ's promise, but it might have languished for lack of truly courageous teachers. A historian of dogma noticed this not so very long ago:

> Christianity could never have conquered the world or become a universal religion if it had not been expressed in terms of the only system of thought which could at that time (the fourth century) claim to be universal. From the religious point of view it could never have overridden the differences between Greek and Barbarian, Jew and Gentile, if it had remained Jewish in its way of thought, if it had not acquired, through contact with the Greek genius, that suppleness which enabled it to reach all systems of thought and all souls. (Tixeront, *History of Dogma*.)

CHAPTER VIII

THE TRINITARIAN FAITH

OF THE EAST

GREEK CATHOLIC THEOLOGY

St Paul's and St John's explanations will be recalled. The
Greek theologians recognized these two as its masters, and in
this lies for us the interest and importance of their writings.
The intellectual climate in which they place us is one of
personal encounter with the three Persons of the Trinity. Just
as Paul and John considered the work of the Father, Son and
Holy Spirit in order to give an idea of the incomprehensible
love of God, so also did the theologians of the Christian East.
But from the description of the rôle of the three Persons in
creation and redemption they rise to the contemplation of their
equality within perfect unity. If the work of each is, if not the
same, at least equal in the divine power that it postulates, it
must inevitably be concluded that the "workers" are consubstantial, one in substance.

In order to explain it better, Greek theology made use of
the theology of *perichoresis*; this is the transcription of a Greek
word which is used to indicate "reciprocity of life", or "community in relationship". Scripture had laid the foundations of
perichoresis. Jesus had said: "Do you believe that I am in the
Father, and the Father is in me?" (John 14. 10; see also 10. 30
and 38). In his turn St Paul declared: "There is no depth in
God's nature so deep that the Spirit cannot find it out" (1 Cor.
2. 10).

Since each of the Persons interpenetrates the others it could be concluded that all three possessed one and the same nature. This Trinity in Unity expressed the mystery of the divine community, which is a mystery of love. The Latins made less use of the theology of *perichoresis*. They thought of God first of all in the unity of his nature and it was in this that they discerned the three Persons, so for them there was no danger of dissolving the divine unity. All the same they kept the Greek ideas. For them *circumincession*, a translation of the Greek *perichoresis*, emphasized the intimacy of the relationship between the three Persons.

The divine Processions: their possibility

In this third part we shall make frequent use of the word "procession"; it is thus necessary to define it.

"Procession" comes from the Latin verb *procedere*, which means to go forward, to pass from one place to another, or from one state to another, but it is also used in the sense in which we say that a thing comes forth or emanates from another, as an object comes from the craftsman who conceived and carried it out. As applied to God it can mean two things:

Firstly that God is the creator, that he is the cause of all created things, which can be explained only by reference to him. Theologians say that it is a procession *ad extra*, or outside God, because it does not affect the divine life. It does not make it either poorer or richer in any way: since God is all-perfect and unchanging, he is neither perfected nor changed by the act of creation. The craftsman, on the other hand, is happy and proud, feels himself more of a man, when he has produced a work of art. This remark alone gives an exact idea of the riches of God's being: all things come from him, but the act of creation in no way changes him, he remains for ever equal in himself. Man's perfection, on the other hand, consists in causing something outside himself. It is only in this way that he can develop his faculties and enrich his being. In giving to the world the fruit of his activity he extends and perfects himself.

Secondly, it is possible to think of another kind of procession in God: one which, although perfectly real remains in himself. Just as in man's intelligence there is a thought which is inherent and constant, and in his will a love which exists there before it is manifested, so in God, a purely spiritual being, it is possible to conceive a thought and a love, which dwell, "proceed" and are born in him. Of such a kind are the processions of the Son and the Holy Spirit. Arius, it will be remembered, lacked this sense of an interior life in God; everything that comes from God, he said, is necessarily exterior to him. So the Word is created. The Greeks protested. Without going as far as the later western teachers they knew that there are processions in God: those of the Father and the Holy Spirit.

Procession and relationship in God

Who "proceeds" in God? The Greeks grasped the truth of it from the first: only the Son and the Holy Spirit can proceed in God. They are the Father's "envoys" in this world, so they are presented as coming from him. On the other hand, since the Father sends and is not sent, he must be the source of all things, even in God. Also, St John says, God is love, life and the principle of life; a life that is for ever poured out in creation, but already in God himself as well. In fact life comes into this world by the two Persons who are its bearers: the Son and the Holy Spirit. (Read again St John 1, 18; 16. 14–15; 17. 4, 6, etc.) But the Father is its source. The other two bring it and make it known, the Father remains enveloped in his silence. He does not come, he does not proceed; on the contrary, all things come from him. On this basis we can understand the individual qualities of the three divine Persons.

The Father

Since the Father is the source in God of all life, we can see that he both has and is the whole nature of God. It is he who communicates it to the Son and the Holy Spirit whom he sent into the world. It is he who is the principle of all things, the source of all "energy", the cause, said the Greeks, of the whole Trinity, the origin of all existence, even the existence of the Son and the Spirit. He is at the pinnacle of the hierarchy of the divine Persons as well as of creation. That is why the Creed at Mass calls him *Patrem omnipotentem, factorem caeli et terrae*: "the Father almighty, creator of heaven and earth."

The Son

It is the Father who begets: his name indicates it and at once demands one who shall be called "Son". The Son, of whom knowledge is given to us by revelation, is the "immediate" term of the divine expansion. There is a first "mission" in God, that of the Son. Jesus had said: "It was from God I took my origin, from him I have come" (John 8. 42). The Greeks develop the idea like this: since the Son was sent on earth *in time*, his generation in eternity must correspond to his "mission" among men. The Father, the eternal spring, eternally begets the stream, which is the Son. The Father, who is eternal intelligence, must also have an eternal *thought*, an eternal *word*. Using images borrowed from the world of material creation, the Greeks could then make use of two different sets of ideas. That of the *eternal generation* was illustrated by the image of the word. That of the *coming* of the Son *in time* made use of the images of Tertullian which were well known to all the Greeks and helped a little to express what the Son is to the Father, but better still they showed the stream of love that comes from the Father.

The Holy Spirit

The third Person is presented to us not as the immediate, but as the *final* term of the divine expansion. The divine vitality in some sense finishes in him as the term which expresses to the full the perfection of the divine being. So the life of the Trinity is resolved "in the Spirit". The outward or "processive" movement which begins in the Father, thus has the Son as its immediate term, but in relation to the Holy Spirit the Son is an "intermediary": the Holy Spirit comes from the Father through the Son. The order of the imparting of divine life thus imposes an *order* in the Trinity and is expressed in the formula, "from the Father through the Son, by the Holy Spirit", that is "all things come from the Father, pass through the Son and find their fulfilment in the Holy Spirit".

Greek theology was well adapted to become a marvellous guide to express for man, the sharer in God's life, the depth of his relationship with God. Thus it was established that the Father is the sole principle[1] of the whole Trinity: that of the Son and of the Spirit. Of the Son—that is clear enough: he is his Father. Of the Holy Spirit—that was more of a difficulty when the Latins declared that the Holy Spirit comes from "Father and Son" (*Filioque*). The Greeks, even when they are Catholics, never think of the divine processions in that way. It is not that they deny the Son a part in the eternal procession of the Holy Spirit, since the procession of the Spirit from the Father by the Son is precisely what they do hold. Yet it is from the Father that he proceeds. In the fourth century St Basil declared: "The Holy Spirit is one, he is revealed as one; he is joined by one Son to one Father, and, in himself, completes the adorable and blessed Trinity" (*Treatise on the Holy Spirit*, 45). In his turn St Athanasius wrote to Serapion: "If the Father creates and renews all things by the Word in the Holy Spirit, what resemblance or relationship is there between creatures and he who creates? . . . If the Son, because he comes from the Father, shares his substance, it necessarily follows that the Spirit also, since he is said to come forth from God, should share the substance of the Son" (*First letter*, 24 and 25).

Another argument is also put forward: since it is admitted that the Holy Spirit possesses sanctifying power of himself, he must be of the same substance as the Son (*First letter*, 20), who, we all know, brings sanctification. St Athanasius added that, since the Spirit has the same power and the same substance as the Son, it is their common life and substance that he brings us.

Such was the light that the fourth century threw on the mystery of the processions and relationships of the divine Persons. But a day came in the ninth century when difficulties arose because Photius, the Patriarch of Constantinople, did not understand the theology of the Greeks, nor that on which the Latins had relied since the time of St Augustine. The essential features of this controversy must now be examined.

[1] A word meaning something which is the origin of another being.

PHOTIUS AGAINST THE CHRISTIAN WEST

St Augustine, in his work of genius, the treatise on the Trinity, departed from the Greek exposition of the subject. The professor from Hippo applied his mind, not to the three divine Persons directly, but to the nature of God, One and Three. At the heart of the divine nature St Augustine distinguished the Person of the Father, of whom the Son is eternally born, holding all that he has and is from the fruitfulness of his Father. But when he turned to the Holy Spirit—and here he parted company with the Greeks—Augustine showed that he proceeds from both Father and Son. How? In the sense—which we shall examine more thoroughly later on—that Father and Son are entranced with love for each other, they meet in a love which is common to both. That love, he said, *is* the Holy Spirit. That is how he proceeds from both. Yet he does not proceed from both in the same way. St Augustine explained with great penetration that the Father remains the one source of the Trinity, and that if the Spirit comes equally from the Son, it is from the Father nonetheless that the Son holds the power to send him forth. This made everything secure. There was basic agreement, though the pattern of presentation was different. Whereas for the Greeks, as we have seen, a line expressed the order of the processions in the Trinity, for Augustine (and later for St Thomas whom he inspired) the equilateral triangle expressed it better. The Father overflows into his Son. Father and Son turn towards each other in mutual love of their common perfection. This movement is expressed by the two angles which incline towards each other to close the form of the triangle; this means that the Holy Spirit is the shared and reciprocated love of Father and Son. Hence the Son, with the Father, is the *principle* of the Holy Spirit, yet not of himself, but only in so far as he derives from the Father the power to be so. In this way the divine hierarchy was secured, with the Father as the source of the whole Trinity.

Basically, this is what the *Filioque* of the Creed at Mass expresses: it was the full normal development of Augustinian theology. To sing at Mass that the Holy Spirit proceeds from the Father *and* the Son does not deny the Father anything, does not make the Son his supplanter. Understood in this way, nothing could better express the faith. But in the ninth century, at the moment when, under Carolingian influence, the *Filioque* was introduced into the Mass, someone was bound to misunderstand it.

The political ambitions of the Patriarch Photius are well known. His whole will was concentrated on seeing that Rome should not be more important than Byzantium. The West was hateful to him. The introduction of the *Filioque* into the Creed was the excuse he needed to provoke a quarrel, which was carried to the point of breaking off relations.

If we are to believe Photius as a theologian, the Holy Spirit proceeds from the Father *alone*. When Scripture declares that the Holy Spirit is the Spirit of the Son as well as the Father (see Rom. 8. 9, 11, etc.) it must be understood, says Photius, in the sense that he is consubstantial with the Son because, like him, he comes from the Father. But the Son has no part in his eternal procession. Here is the design of his explanation:

The Father is at the summit. From him comes the Son by way of generation and the Holy Spirit by way of procession. It is clear from this that the relationship between Son and Holy Spirit consists entirely in the fact that both come from the Father. That is all they have in common.

But Photius' explanation was also meant to be controversial. He needed to prove that the Latins were in error, so he hurled at them an accusation of heresy. The Latins, he said, hold that the Spirit proceeds from Father and Son as from two independent principles. The Holy Spirit is in some way the point of convergence of Father and Son, but they are not united in his procession. Hence they do not form *one principle* from which the Holy Spirit proceeds; they are merely united in him.

This was a serious accusation, and it seemed to place the Latins in the heretical camp. In fact, Photius was a hundred miles away from St Augustine's theology, but the Latins had to pay the price of his ignorance, or rather it was the unity of the Church that paid it, for the schism became complete. It was to last a long time, for it still exists.

CHAPTER IX

ONE AND THREE

THE DIVINE COMMUNITY IN THE WESTERN MIND

There are three Persons in one God. Each possesses one and the same nature. That is the teaching of faith, and we must see now how the Latins explained it. The masters in this subject are St Augustine and St Thomas. The difficulty lies in showing in what sense the Trinity, as Tertullian had already said, can constitute the divine Unity. We must move in thought from the One God, the absolute, to the Three-in-One, whose mystery lies in the relationship one to another of the Persons.

THE ETERNAL PROCESSIONS

The definition of "procession" which was given in the previous chapter is of primary importance to the Latins, the theologians of God's interior life. First of all, to dispose of false problems, we must answer this question: what is there in God that cannot be said to proceed? After that it will be easier to discuss the Son and the Holy Spirit, who alone *do* proceed.

The divine nature, obviously, does not proceed. If it did then it would itself have to derive from some other, preexisting nature, which would be absurd, so that we would end by talking of two divine natures, and thus of two Gods. As we have seen, Scripture never once says that the Father was sent among men. Our professions of faith proclaim him "The Father who is derived from no other" (Lyons, 1274). "The Father, all that he is and has he holds from no other, but from himself, he is the principle without a principle" (Florence, 1442). On this point Greeks and Latins have never disagreed; but the theologian investigates further. He throws light on the first divine Person by analysing the names traditionally reserved to him of Father, Principle, Unbegotten.

The Father

⟨This name is given to him by the Gospel as the fitting name for him of whom we say that he is at the summit of the divinity. In addition, Scripture tells us that this Father has a Son. Yet nowhere is it said that the Father is himself the son of a father. In the eyes of faith, we know, such a statement would be meaningless: there is but one Son of God. The name Father reveals at once a Person without origin. To speak of the Father is to say that he who bears the name has a son, but it does not require that he himself should be a son, that is, that he should derive his being from another. Paternity is a quality that indicates the mysterious fecundity of one person as the source of other beings; it does not mean that this person himself has an origin.

The Principle

The old documents of the faith proclaim that the Father is the principle, that is, the starting-point of the whole Trinity. To say that he is a principle is to affirm at the same time that other beings find their origin in him. Principle, then, is a name that completes the previous one: to be a father means to give life, and so to be the principle of other, and like, persons. But what is a Principle without a principle? That is the mystery of the first Person, so rich in his own being that it is easier to see what comes from him than the fact that he himself does not come from anyone.

The Unbegotten

This name completes the others. It implies the lack of origin, the absence of dependence on anyone at all. Unbegotten leads us to consider the Father in his condition as fatherless, that is as not-being-a-son, but not as without a son, since the

Unbegotten is also the Father. Briefly, Unbegotten is a name that refers to the Father as absolutely transcendent, rather than as generative which was the aspect of him evoked by the two preceding names. The Unbegotten—a name unfathomable, impenetrable, to creatures who long to see into the origin of all beings. Only the first two speak to us of his fecundity, which is what we have next to consider.

An impressive train of thought lies behind the Latin theology of the processions. It appeals to the world of the mind, of human psychology. Then, by means of analogy, we can say that what is true of man can be applied to God, in an infinitely higher manner.

Man, according to the sacred writings, is made in the image of God. It follows that whatever is most noble in him must be able to express something of God. But man is spiritual—that is his greatest distinction. It is, then, permissible to conclude that the powers of the spirit, intelligence and will must also be found in God. Certain consequences follow from this.

Father and Son: the Thought and its Utterance

St John called Jesus the Son of God, the only Son, *the Word* (Prologue and 1. 18). St Paul called Jesus the Wisdom of God (1 Cor. 1. 24). These two names given to the Son of God were the rough draft of the great theology that St Augustine and later St Thomas were one day to perfect. The Son of God, according to Scripture, comes from an intellectual region: he is the Word or Utterance of God. It follows that the Father who begets the Son must be a mind capable of thought. Also we are faced here with the law of spirits whose primary function is to "think". But in man the interior utterance, by which he tells himself about things of which he is aware, is very weak. A word, a breath, is all he can express, and it is gone immediately. There is nothing constant, nothing "substantial" about it. Its existence, even, is not a necessity—it could well not be. It is, as the philosophers say, "accidental".

But in spite of this my interior utterance is not unimportant. When I think this interior concept expresses exactly the state of my mind at that moment, both its content and what it is in itself. Really, concretely, my mind is expressed by my concept or utterance, it is at that moment its perfect expression. It is, we might suggest, "consubstantial" with it.

We must transfer these ideas and apply them to God. First we have the non-proceeding Person, the Father. But the Father is God and possesses all the divine mind. The Father, then, is a mind capable of thought. Since he is perfect, perfect also is his act of knowledge. This, then, is the Word, without flaw, an exact reproduction of the Father, "bearing the stamp of his substance", his perfect, sufficient, substantial expression. The Word of God the Father is, then, of the same nature as the Father, and not in any "accidental" way. He is God as the Father is, "of one substance with the Father", a living Person. He himself does not beget, because in his act of utterance the Father expressed the whole of divinity (and all creation) so there is nothing left to express or beget. Hence it is impossible that the Son should be the Father, or even that he should be *a* father. He is the begotten, the one in whom the Father utters himself completely, the one in whom the Father sees all the beings that he wills to create, all that creation which is, by that fact, made in the image of the Word.

Moreover the Word is Son because he proceeds from the Father alone, in the way that a human son proceeds from his father, meaning that he bears his likeness. Intelligence is wonderful in that it comes to resemble that which it contemplates. It is even true to say that it can understand nothing unless it becomes the other through resembling it. For man, to understand a thing means, in a way, to become that thing. It means, Claudel would say, to share its birth. This is the wonder that leads to union, and it is one that takes place on the spiritual plane. But the divine intelligence does not suffer from the human need to reach out to another being in order to know it; when the Father expresses himself totally in his Word he gives birth eternally to a whole, like himself. And the Word-Son necessarily remains united to his Father, since he is his exact image, the expression of his nature. The Son is son because he is Word, and the Word, because he is begotten of the Father, is the Son, "the true likeness of the God we cannot see" (Col. 1. 15).

There is enough in this to give many an earthly father food for thought. It refers to his power of procreation, yet it is an imperfect power, the son that a father begets is not his exact likeness, above all he does not attain to that degree of personal perfection that all fathers would like for their sons. First of all he is born as a child, far from man's estate. For many long years the father, with the help of the mother who was necessary to the procreation of their son, must provide for his education as the normal continuation of the act of procreation. That is what education means: a father and mother want to give their son by stages all that they could not communicate to him when they brought him into the world. God acts out of his superabundance, and expresses himself all at once, in his eternal act of generation. Earthly parents need time to make of their son a man, a complete human being, and God himself unceasingly gives him the grace he needs in order to become "the image of his Son" (Rom. 8. 29).

The Holy Spirit, the breath of love

We have revealed one first act in God: that of intelligence. Its term was the Word-Son. But the idea of spirit demands a second act. When a man has conceived a good and beautiful piece of work, his whole soul goes out to it, he loves it. Hence the second act or procession in God is that of desire or love. But it is immediately apparent that if the Father alone sufficed to bring forth his Word this no longer applies when we consider his love. Love of its nature demands an object towards which it may reach out. But to whom could the Father reach out if not to the Son who mirrors all his perfection? With a single impulse he inclines to the Son whom he begets eternally, and rests in him, for he loves him who is infinitely lovable, the Son to whom he has communicated the whole of the divine nature (and in the same impulse he loves the creature which he sees in his Son). So the first impulse of love is that of the Father towards his Son. But the Word, who is the knowledge of all things, knows the Father's love for him. He knows also that the Father's love belongs to him. The Word knows and keeps for himself what is his. But also, with the same impulse of love which the Father has for him, and which he makes his own, he turns back to the Father in order to return it to him in an act of thanksgiving. So the love of Father and Son is common to both; to be more exact, it is the *same* love, and it means that Father and Son, inclined towards each other, find ecstasy in each other, as two beings who love one another and tell their love one to another.

But this love is in God. It is quite a different matter from our poor human love, for it subsists in him. It is the divine nature uniting Father and Son, the divine nature proceeding from them, going from one to another, as love. This subsistent love is the Holy Spirit, of whom Saint Bernard said that he is "the kiss exchanged between Father and Son".

Why is he called the Holy Spirit? St Thomas Aquinas explains that he is called the Spirit because he proceeds from the Father *and* the Son by a sort of shared and uniting breath (the theologians call it a "spiration"). And he is called "Holy" because all things are called holy which are consecrated to God. Love proceeds from Father and Son joined together in the unity of love, forming in their two selves but one single principle, so the Holy Spirit proceeds from *both Father and Son*. In this way the faith of the Creed is explained and reason is satisfied: "The Father and the Son", says St Thomas, "have but one single power of spiration, identical in number; that is why the Holy Spirit proceeds equally from both of them" (*Summa Theologica*, 1. 36, 2, solution 2). But we must remember that it is from the Father that the Son derives his power of spiration. At this point we have reached the term, the end, of the divine processions. Faith teaches it, reason subscribes to it.

THE MISSIONS OF THE SON AND THE HOLY SPIRIT IN TIME

Theologians would never have been able or have dared to penetrate so far into the mystery of God, would not have dreamed even of lifting their eyes to the eternal processions of the Son and the Holy Spirit, if Scripture had not led them to do so. Not that Scripture has anything at all to say about the eternal processions, but in imparting to us its teaching on the salvation of the human race it proclaimed that it was the Son and the Holy Spirit who, coming forth from the Father, had brought it to us. From contemplating their "sending" into this world theologians concluded that the mystery of God corresponded to the way of salvation: the sending or mission in time of a divine Person supposes his parallel and eternal procession from the Father. It follows from this that only those Persons who proceed are "sent", and in fact the Father, known to be without origin, is never described as being sent. The whole of the first part of this book—the chapters on St Paul and St John in particular—was devoted to examining the missions of the Son and the Spirit. Here it will only be necessary to clarify a few details.

The missions of the Son and the Spirit are of two kinds: *visible* when the invisible Person who is sent takes on a visible form of presence in this world. The eternal Word-Son appeared in visible form in his Incarnation, the Holy Spirit took a bodily shape at the baptism of Jesus and the appearance of tongues of fire on the day of Pentecost. It is noticeable that the visible form shows the effect that God wished to produce. God made himself human in the Son who took on our visible shape. On the day of Jesus' baptism he showed what power lay in the Messias and showed him to be under the protection of the Most High, in some sense made fruitful by the Holy Spirit as were the waters of Genesis in the days of creation (Gen. 1. 2). The tongues of fire were evidently a sign of the love and power of witness—greatest of the Spirit's gifts—which were made manifest in the apostles from that moment.

The *invisible* missions mean that the divine Persons adopt a new and unseen mode of presence in this world. Of this kind is the indwelling of God in the souls of the just. It is more than a deification, it is a real indwelling in them of the Three. We need only recall the words of Jesus: "If a man has any love for me, he will be true to my word; and then he will win

my Father's love, and we will both come to him and make
our continual abode with him" (John 14. 23). Or again: "That
while thou art in me I am in them" (John 17. 23). And on the
presence of the Son in the Christian see also Gal. 2. 20; Rom.
8. 10; Ephes. 3. 17. The invisible presence of the Holy Spirit
in the Christian is dealt with in 1 Cor. 6. 19; 12. 11; Gal. 4. 6.

These are the statements in Scripture which it is the theologian's task to explain. But enough has been said here to
show that for us the mystery of the Trinity is an incentive to
very deep thought on the condition of man, raised even to the
level of divine life and familiar friendship with God, called to
share in the communion of the three Persons.

THE THREE DIVINE PERSONS AND THE MYSTERY OF THEIR ETERNAL RELATIONSHIPS

The eternal birth of the Son and the mysterious procession of
the Spirit, the shared love of Father and Son, tell us that God
is a living God. They also emphasize the order of origin among
the Persons and their hierarchy. Take away the ideas of movement, order, origin, or procession in God: nothing is left but
the three Persons, eternally face to face with each other, each
related to the others. They are perfect entities harmoniously
united among themselves within that one nature which is
possessed equally by each. It is the mystery of the relations
between the divine Persons, God's mystery itself. If man is
made in the image of God, to learn about the divine Persons
will also teach us something about personality itself and about
all human relationships.

The divine "relations"

Nowadays when we talk about "relation" we are on familiar
ground. Contemporary thought is used to the word since the
scientific theories of Einstein, and historical science also has
helped us to get a better grasp of how men and events are
"conditioned". Everything is relative, people say, meaning that
a fact can only be accurately interpreted when it is seen in its
proper context.

But the theologian makes use of the word "relation" more than most people. Without it he cannot talk about God at any length. It is not that God could equally well not be, or be other than he is. The theologian speaking of God needs to make use of the idea of *relation* because without this notion he cannot enter deeply into the subject of the divine life. What we have to attempt now is to define "relation" and then to apply the idea to the divine Being, or, to be exact, to each of the divine Persons—Father, Son and Holy Spirit—three Persons whose life consists in being relative each to the others.

Relation, in its most important sense, expresses the connection between two beings united by a special bond. When I say that Peter is John's father I am asserting the existence between Peter and John of a relation in virtue of which Peter is connected with John by paternity, and John with Peter by filiation. Being in paternal relation to John means that Peter is orientated towards him and that his life as "father" finds its meaning only in John's existence. All his being as father belongs to John. In his turn John is orientated towards Peter, not as a stranger but as a son.

This is already enough to indicate the mystery of the bonds which unite men. Nothing could be falser than to conclude, as people do nowadays, that there is therefore absolute equality between them. Certainly equality must be maintained in one aspect of the matter: John is Peter's equal in that they are both men. On the plane of human nature, which is identical in Peter and John, they have an equal value. This is true also on a worldwide scale: it is one of the great achievements of Christianity that it has for so long taught that men are equal in spite of race and colour. But equality is not the same thing as egalitarianism. An invisible order is established between Peter and John and between John and Peter. Peter, to whom John owes his origin, will always be his superior, and, if he understands what it means to be a son, John will regard Peter who begot him with respect and gratitude all his life. The son is the lesser of the two because it is the father who gave him life and to whom therefore he owes everything. It was exactly in this sense that Jesus once said: "My Father has greater power than I" (John 14. 28), greater because it is he who begot him. But Peter will not make use of his superiority to crush his son; he will be a true father to him, keeping a loving watch over his life. Since he has bestowed his whole human nature on him he will continue his work as a father by developing his son's talents and abilities. He will work lovingly and without thought of self, through abnegation and sacrifice, never ceasing to wear himself out, to give all that he has, in order to bring his son to his full manhood. The mystery of fatherhood is the mystery of self-giving. The father's superiority lies only in his capacity for giving himself more completely.

All this will help us to a clear view of the divine life, but all the elements which we see repeated here are present in infinite perfection. Peter is certainly a father, John is really a son, but Peter's fatherhood is not essential to him: he could have been simply a man without ever begetting. So Peter is not necessarily a father, we can say he is a father *accidentally*, meaning that it is not necessarily part of his nature to have a son. But since he is a father he is enriched by it, his manhood is perfected. Is this what happens in God? Certainly not. God is eternally a Father because his Son is eternal. There is nothing "accidental" about God, everything in him is essential to him. Fatherhood does not just happen to him, as it does to a man, for God is necessarily and substantially a Father. Fatherhood is the very substance of God, that is why it is a person. In Peter, fatherhood is a relationship which is added to him. In God, Fatherhood is God himself, God the Father, but not God the Son.

God the Son is the relation of sonship. God the Holy Spirit is the relation of "Love-between-Father-and-Son". There is, then, "relationship" in God, but in it each of the divine Persons can be discerned.

It follows that, since relationship in God *is* God, and since there are three related Persons in God, Father, Son and Holy Spirit, then each of them (although related to each of the others) is God too. This confirms the truth of the mystery of God, One in nature but Three in Persons. Far from being an affirmation of the existence of three Gods the mystery of the

Trinity lies in the existence of a trinity of relations or relationships in one God, and each of these is itself God since it possesses the whole of the divine essence. Each one is God, yet the three are one God only.

But the three Persons can only be understood and distinguished by means of the qualities proper to each. To the Father belongs fatherhood since it is he who begets. But we must not imagine from this a God who exists completely in a knowledge of himself: if he is a father he must have a son. This Son is eternally begotten and beloved in the Father. And since lastly there is the Holy Spirit in God, God the Holy Spirit must be the kin of Father and Son, with his proper existence, the living breath of love between them. The whole mystery of personality consists in the fact that a subject with its own fixed qualities can have a necessary relationship with another subject. This is a question that must now be discussed.

Divine Personality

In his *Summa Theologica* St Thomas Aquinas defines personality in this way: "Personality signifies the most perfect thing in the whole of nature: namely, what subsists in a rational nature" (1, 29, 3).

This definition implies three qualities. *Incommunicability*, the distinguishing mark of all beings: it means that one is not another and is entirely distinct from another. The Father is not the Son because to beget is the power proper to him whereas it is proper to the Son to be begotten. *Subsistence*, existence as a complete and perfect being: every individual subsists, but a part of an individual has no subsistence. An arm does not subsist, it is not an individual, so we cannot attribute any action to it; we attribute it to the individual who performed it "with his arm". When the individual is a conscious personality it has the third quality of *intellectuality*. A being lacking this quality can only be vegetable or animal. Its possession places it among rational beings: man, angel or God. Intellectuality makes the individual *conscious*, master of his actions, capable of thought and desire, able to enter into relationships with other beings, and of realizing a duty towards them. The reverse

process is equally valid: the rational individual is the object
of the rights and duties of others. That is the natural law.
It emphasizes the intellectual character of the individual in
virtue of which he is called a person.

To sum up, human personality implies the perfection of a
nature endowed with intelligence and free will, called to develop
its powers through actions proper to its order in the realm of
conscience and morality. Again, a being cannot be a person
unless, out of the riches of its own nature it is capable of acts
which bring it into contact with other created beings.

On the strength of this analysis it is safe to assert that the
Father, Son and Holy Spirit are Persons. Each is distinct from
the others, each subsists in a manner proper to itself within
the divine nature; consequently each one is intelligence and
will. As Christians we are no longer simply called to contemplate the one God—the oneness of God is in his nature—
instead we are offered the vision of a three-personed God.
Three Persons subsisting in One nature, all three being in
themselves intelligence and will, since intelligence and will are
the marks of the purely spiritual being of God. God, three and
one, is the origin of all things, their creator. It is he who dwells
in us by grace and by his real presence. One God, making
divine by his nature, guest of our souls as Three-in-One: flowing from the mystery of God in himself, such is the mystery
of the Trinity in us.

CHAPTER X

THEOLOGY AND SPIRITU-ALITY: THE DIVINE PERSONS AND HUMAN SOCIETY

THE MYSTERY OF DIVINE PERSONALITY

Everything encourages us to follow up our inquiries about God, to attempt to gain further vital knowledge. In doing so we shall take the particular point of view from which each Person is seen as "for the sake of the others". We shall explore still further the wonderful vistas that St Augustine and St Thomas opened up to us in the last chapter. Here it is not so much the incommunicability of each Person that we shall examine as the "ecstatic" relationship between them. Incommunicability is sufficient to prevent any confusion between Father, Son and Holy Spirit; what is important here is the "ecstasy", that is, the overflowing into another, the Father giving himself to the Son, the return that the Son makes the Father, the thanksgiving of the Spirit to Father and Son. Each of these three reveals love to us.

The Father, the pure gift of Self

"Source of the whole Trinity"—thus the old documents of the Church proclaim him. The Father is that mysterious Person who possesses the whole divine nature without having received it, and communicates it to the Son and the Holy Spirit. Without origin, yet originator of all; receiving nothing, yet giver of all; giving all that he is yet losing nothing that he has; fruitful, origin of the whole Trinity and of the whole created universe—above all Father of a Son. The name of "Father" conjures up in our minds, as yet unprepared for it, not the solitude of a God without relationships but the eternal communication of himself to his Son: "The Father's being can only be explained in relation to the Son", said the Council of Toledo long ago. The Son is begotten with all the Father's own perfections, of a fatherhood so perfect that it is completely expressed in bringing forth this only Son, who must therefore be the Father's exact image. And the love which the Father bears the Son and also shares with the Son to whom he has given all his love—even to the very power of loving—from this love springs the Holy Spirit, the pledge that God is indeed all love. So the Father has a double relationship; he is Father of a Son, and he also "breathes forth" the Spirit which is the kiss of their mutual self-giving.

The Father also knows all created things in the World. He wills them so that they may show forth his glory and eminence. It is necessary to him to beget the Word, the Father's own being is impossible without him, but creation is quite another matter. Far from being necessary to him creation only exists because he has willed it. This alone shows that in creating God was under no compulsion but that of Love. It is in love that he communicates his own overflowing abundance, making all things a reflection of himself.

The Father, The End-Purpose of Revelation

The Father is also Silence. We know that he has not spoken, for he has never been among us, but he has revealed himself in his Son and continues to reveal himself through the Spirit of them both. The Son and the Spirit are, then, the revelation of the Father in an exact sense.

The Father's revelation through the Son is quite clear. Since he is the Word of the Father, his perfect expression, his image, the human words that the Son poured forth among men were the revelation in time not so much of himself as of the Father. St John emphasizes this on the first page of his Gospel: "No man has even seen God [the Father]; but now his only-begotten Son, who abides in the bosom of the Father, has himself become our interpreter" (1. 18).

And one day when Philip said to him: "Lord, let us see the Father, that is all we ask", Jesus replied: "What, Philip, here am I who have been all this time in your company; hast thou not learnt to recognize me yet? Whoever has seen me has seen the Father; what dost thou mean by saying, Let us see the Father?" (John 14. 8–9).

In fact the whole Gospel bears witness that Jesus came on earth to tell us about the Father in heaven. His sermon on the mountain of the Beatitudes proves this: it presents not so much a moral code as a practical attitude that we ought to adopt in the sight of our heavenly Father (Matt. 5–7). But surely the most important text, one to which we should return, is the cry of exultation in which Christ communicates to us the secret of his joy and invites us to share it. His Soul was steeped in the vision of the Father. Through humility, by the "way" which is himself, we may come to the Father: "Father, who art lord of heaven and earth, I give thee praise that thou hast hidden all this from the wise and prudent, and revealed it to little children. Be it so, Father, since this finds favour in thy sight. My Father has entrusted everything into my hands; none knows the Son truly except the Father, and none knows the Father truly except the Son, and those to whom it is the Son's good pleasure to reveal him" (Matt. 11. 25–7).

It was of the Father that Jesus spoke when he was teaching. He taught us that he was Love for us and that he proved his love by giving us his Son (John 3. 16; see 11. 41). In the staggering prayer recorded in John 17, Jesus reveals once more the Father's will to unite all men to himself through his Son.

To know him is to possess eternal life. Those who will not receive him remain in the darkness of sin, for "Whatever gifts are worth having, whatever endowments are perfect of their kind, these come to us from above; they are sent down by the Father of all that gives light, with whom there can be no change, no swerving from his course" (James 1. 17).

So the Father remained in his mysterious transcendence, for it was not his will to appear, but his Son came to tell us about him, and did it so effectively that our hearts are still on fire, or at least are alerted to the need to search for him.

But now the Father also reveals himself through the Holy Spirit living in the Church. If, as St John tells us, the Spirit bears witness to the Son this does not indicate that his teaching mission is confined to communicating the meaning of Christ: the Spirit brings us the revelation of the Son in its entirety, which must include the revelation of the Father: "The Holy Spirit . . . will in his turn make everything plain, and recall to your minds everything that I have said to you" (John 14. 26).

It is to the Father that both Son and Holy Spirit turn: the Son tells his Father that he has accomplished the mission he has entrusted to him (John 17. 4–6 and 22–4); the Spirit plants in the hearts of the faithful a spirit befitting adopted sons, so that they may both know and cry out to their Father in heaven (Rom. 8. 15–16; Gal. 4. 6).

It is towards the Father that Christ's whole life tends; it is to him that he was going, passing to him from this world (John 13. 1 and 17. 1–5). It is also towards him that the Spirit directs us now. The Spirit of adoption that he has given to us draws us back to the Father: "The Spirit himself thus assures our spirit that we are children of God; and if we are his children, then we are his heirs too; heirs of God, sharing the inheritance of Christ; only we must share his sufferings if we are to share his glory" (Rom. 8. 16–17).

We cannot escape the obligation to prove this by our actions. Our works, like those of Christ's earthly life, must make it evident that there is a Father in heaven: "and your light must shine so brightly before men that they can see your good works, and glorify your Father who is in heaven" (Matt. 5. 16).

In this spiritual context sin acquires a new meaning. Sin is strictly our work and, as such, powerless to discover anything about the Father. On the contrary, it tends to lessen the revelation. It is the reverse of this that we hear in the voice of the aged Ignatius of Antioch who, living in the Spirit and longing to be conformed with Christ through martyrdom, declared that he no longer cared for earthly things. He had surrendered to the spirit of sonship, which bred in him the desire to return to his Father's house. And so he wrote to the Romans (7. 12). There is nothing beyond the Father. The secret for a Christian lies in discovering something of him.

The Son, he who receives with humility

Our Promethean age[1] would be quite willing to take the Father's place. Nor would it do so simply in order to give without thought of self—the vice of paternalism is too deeply rooted in it—but it is even further from any resemblance to the Son.

The Word is Son because he is *the expression of the Father*. Far from being the Unbegotten, the source of life, he is simply the "Image", the reproduction of the Father. "What the Son is, he is only by receiving it from the Father", said the Council of Toledo. But, if we may put it like this, it is because he is willing to exist not of himself but by another that he possesses —receiving them from that other—the fullness of *glory*, *grace* and *truth* (John 1. 14). From this we can see the Son's position: he is all humility because he has received all, he is begotten of God the Father, owing his existence to the Father's fecundity. Certainly the Trinity is a trinity of equals; the Three share one and the same nature; but a hierarchy is established at the heart of this equality. Only one is the absolute gift of self—the Father; the Son is primarily docile and passive—he receives everything. It is only following on this that he gives himself back to his Father with an ecstatic impulse, the impulse of gratitude and love, a love that is fruitful. But he only

[1] The Myth of Prometheus signifies the superman's desire to make himself god.

loves after he has received. This is also the case with the Holy Spirit, but he receives without bearing fruit within God.

The Son, the High Priest

We have already explained that he who is in the relationship of loving passivity to the Father owes it to himself to reproduce in a sinful world—a world that can only make a mock of the source of love—his own attitude to eternity. So it is that when he took the human form that made him a man as we are in the womb of the Virgin Mary, he was consecrated as High Priest. There grew in his human soul a love that was expressed in prayer, a sacrificial love that rose up to the Father from this world of sin. His filial love inspired this return to God, the Father, but—and this was the purpose of his coming—sinful humanity was drawn in its wake. His purpose was not only to save humanity but to give it back to the Father. This was the temporal task of the eternal Son. Humility breeds obedience: "What I do is always what pleases him" (John 8. 29); both reach their consummation in redemptive love. This was the origin and the completion of the "sacrifice of the Head". All those whom the Father knew in his Son (Rom. 8. 29) and whom he would one day entrust to him, all these the Son sacrificed in his own person, so that they might be perfectly made one in the life of God (John 17. 6 and 19–24). In this way was realized the vocation of all created things; all were formed once more into praise and thanksgiving to God.

So the redemption of man—which is his re-creation—is in perfect harmony with his first creation: all things are made through the Word, the eternal Son and High Priest of mankind; all things bear his seal, even that created universe in which he once took root through his human flesh. What can put bounds to the love of God—except our sins which are its negation? The wonderful thing about the Virgin Mary, the thing which makes her a never outworn example for Christians, is that she, like her Son, was full of humility and dependence on the Father: "He who is mighty, he whose name is holy, has wrought for me his wonders. . . . He has put down the mighty from their seat, and exalted the lowly" (Luke 1. 49–51).

The Son as the model of the Christian

The Son, the Word of God, with the Holy Spirit alone knows the Father, is alone the witness of his eternal glory (John 1. 14), his only true witness on earth (John 17. 6). If all creation is made in his image then the Christian has a higher claim to bear that image and so he must reproduce in himself the features of the Son. On the subject of this mystical imitation of Christ St Thomas has left us some wonderful lines in a famous commentary on the Apostles' creed.

If the Word of God is the Son of God, if all God's words are in the likeness of this Word, we must above all listen to God's words. For the sign of our love for God is to be willing to listen to his words. Then, we must believe God's words; only in this way can the Word of God live in us—the Christ, the Word of God: "May Christ dwell by faith in your hearts. But you have not the Word of God dwelling in you." But we should also meditate on the Word of God dwelling in us, for it is not enough to believe, we must meditate, otherwise the Word will avail us nothing; and this meditation is a priceless weapon against sin: "I have hidden thy Word in my heart to meditate on it so that I might not sin against thee." And again it is said of the just man: "He meditates on the law of the Lord day and night." It is said of the Blessed Virgin that she "kept in her heart the memory of all this". In addition, a man must *communicate* the Word of God to his fellows by counsel and preaching, inflaming their hearts with love: "Let no evil words come from your mouth, but good words, to edification. May all the wealth of Christ's inspiration have its shrine among you; now you will have instruction and advice for one another." "Preach the Gospel, bear witness in season and out of season." Finally the Word of God must be put into *practice*: "Be ye doers of the word and not hearers only, deceiving yourselves."

The Holy Spirit, the pinnacle of the divine unity

"If we are right to think that the Father gives, and the Son receives, the kiss, then we shall not be mistaken in saying that the kiss itself is the Holy Spirit, that is, the one who is, between Father and Son, the unchanging peace, the fast-binding cement, the undivided love, the inseparable unity" (St Bernard, *Sermons on the Song of Songs*).

The Holy Spirit, then, is the eternal Person who can only be explained by love. It follows that he is the pledge that God is Love. All three Persons are love but only he can prove it, since his eternal rôle is to give expression to it. And if he is Love, he can show us most perfectly what love is. Love, like the Holy Spirit, is first of all complete passivity: he is the result of a gift, after being the gift itself. The Holy Spirit is Love because he alone receives all that he is from the Father and the Son. As we have already said, in God the Spirit who is Love has himself no fecundity, for nothing proceeds from him. But this passivity has a wonderful meaning: it is the praise of glory in God, the inner glory of God. From all eternity the Holy Spirit is wrapped in the ecstasy of Father and Son; returning towards them, loving them as he must because he is their mutual love; he yearns towards them, loving them of necessity because he has received love from them. His fruitfulness is in the Church, and this also comes to him only from the Two.

The love of renunciation in fruitful activity

The Holy Spirit, unfruitful in God, is the fruitfulness of the Church. In the Acts of the Apostles the Holy Spirit is seen coming to enrich the Church with God's gifts. But there is no need to look far for the mark of perfect love; it is "agape". This word means love that gives itself without demanding anything in return, love which cares only for the good of the beloved. But love of this kind does not wish to boast of its own fecundity, but rather that of him who gave it. He who really loves, with a love that comes from God, seeks to be unseen so that no one shall think that he is the author of his own abundance; on the contrary, he wants everyone to know that it comes to him from God. This is the very opposite of pride. Love with humility does not glorify itself, but glorifies by its works him who gave the power to perform them.

So it is with the Spirit. His activity is directed towards another. He proclaims the Son's meaning, he bears him witness (John 15. 26), he glorifies him (John 16. 14).

He does not do this of himself—Jesus tells us this—but because he has heard and received the message he must give (John 16. 13–14). He gives men knowledge of the Son in order to bring them to the Father:

> Per te sciamus da Patrem
> Noscamus atque Filium.

> Through thee may we the Father know,
> Through thee the eternal Son.
> *(Veni Creator Spiritus.)*

The Spirit makes even this possible for us. In the Church the Spirit is Love-for-us, the gift of Father and Son: "The Holy Spirit whom the Father will send on my account" (John 14. 26). He is their activity among us, their continuation here on earth. It is he also who puts love into our hearts, for he himself is love. "The love of God has been poured out in our hearts by the Holy Spirit whom we have received" (Rom. 5. 5).

He is the spiritual wealth of the Christian, it is he who forms him into God by the love which he pours out in him. He is the gift which is given to the poor in spirit: *Pater pauperum.* He is the creator of a new life: "heal that which is sick". He is the blessed light that guides our steps, he is the stream that flows from the Father to shape the world into one again.

MAN IN THE IMAGE OF GOD

> What is man that thou shouldst remember him?
> What is Adam's breed that it should claim thy care?
> Thou hast placed him only a little below the angels,
> crowning him with glory and honour (Psalm 8. 5–6).

Communication with God

God, the author of man, made him in his own likeness. By this very fact links are forged between them. But man must not rest content with a purely human state. In order to remain God's living image man must bind himself anew to God from moment to moment. "If God does not exist, am I still the master?" cried one of the heroes in *The Possessed*. Dostoevski was right: man is only man as long as he acknowledges

God as the author of his whole life. To be a subsistent person does not do away with the need to maintain contact with God. It is by a willingness to submit to the action of his Creator and Saviour that a man becomes a living person, made in God's image.

First, then, there must be submission to God's action. Man does not live by doing a lot of things, by working and giving, but by receiving God and by giving himself to him. The source of all life is the Blessed Trinity. St Augustine has left us a record of an experience of this which cannot be challenged. The great rhetorician from Hippo was shaken by love and fear when he knew the living God for the first time by direct experience. He knew himself to be far from him who is "eternal truth", "true love", "beloved eternity", an exile in a strange land that knew not God, where he existed but as a shadow and a ghost:

"O eternal truth and true love and beloved eternity! Thou art my God, I sigh to thee by day and by night. When first I knew thee, thou didst lift me up so that I might see that there was something to see, but that I was not yet the man to see it. And thou didst beat back the weakness of my gaze, blazing upon me too strongly, and I was shaken with love and with dread. And I knew that I was far from thee in the region of unlikeness" (*Confessions*, 7, 10). He had thought himself rich in human gifts, but, instead, his exile from God had cramped him. Then he realized that man's perfection can only be found in his nearness to God.

More recently Romano Guardini gave a warning that the increase in technical skill was being accompanied by a weakening of moral strength. He found the explanation in man's independence of God:

One gets the impression that man's moral strength weakens in the proportion that his power increases, and that there is a space where the personality ought to be. It cannot be otherwise, for man is not a person existing of himself, who as such could enter or not enter into a relationship with God, as he pleased; but his personality only exists in this very relationship. In detaching himself from God he becomes impersonal, and the contrast between what man can be and what he is contributes to his critical position. Man has sinned by separating his power from God; it is this power itself which will be the instrument of his punishment.

We must understand him rightly: it is not technical skill itself that spoils the moral powers, but the fact that by means of them man wants to become equal with God. It is the drama of the garden of Eden, in the book of Genesis. It is the present-day drama of atheistic humanism. To refuse God is to establish oneself in a condition of the most absolute independence. The expected coming of the superman shows just how far contempt for God can go. The horrors of recent wars, and the still more horrible ones that modern weapons might let loose on our planet, are a proof of this that makes us tremble. If God does not exist, anything is permissible to his supplanter. And we can see that the worm of atheism which has settled in the hearts of our generation is leading the despairing disciples of Nietzsche and of Jean-Paul Sartre towards the suppression of the self. Without God there is nothing to aim at, and no need for that reverent care for others which gives birth to love.

Without God also man is sick. One of the useful things that present-day psychiatry has taught us is that certain neuroses spring from the fact that some limited human values or ideas —such as "superman", "unbridled liberty", "unrestrained pleasure" or human love regarded as the end of life—are made a substitute for God. When God is removed from the centre of man's being his psychology is upset, his personality becomes exhausted, dissolves, even to the point of serious illness and certain forms of madness. To come from another, said Pius XII, is to be in a necessary relationship to that other. It shows that man cannot explain himself apart from God, and that no one can ignore with impunity the force that impels him towards the source of his being (From a discourse to a Catholic International Congress on Psychotherapy, 1953).

The human mind demands an inner unity if it is to be properly balanced. But it is obvious that its Creator willed that this unity should only be possible through preliminary union with himself. But it is only in Christ Jesus, through whom all things were made, and by whom all is recovered and recreated, that all things take on once more the likeness of God: "Just as God, in giving us life, gave us also this world and ourselves, so, in giving us Jesus as our life, God once more gave us to ourselves" (Bérulle).

That is the reason why the saints were such great personalities: they were always conscious of the source of their being and unceasingly renewed themselves in it. "Sanctity is the one hope of man," cried Abbé Blanchard in an essay on "Sanctity today". Sanctity, or the struggle towards it, is the only state which makes God present to us: "And see, all of a sudden you are someone" (Claudel).

And St Thomas explains in his turn:

> Alone among creatures the rational nature is directly regulated with reference to God. The reason is that other creatures do not reach the universal but only the particular level; they share in God's perfection either simply by existing (as in the case of inanimate creatures) or else by living and knowing particular, individual things (as in the case of plants and animals). A rational nature, on the other hand, in the measure in which it has a knowledge of the good and of being from a universal point of view, finds itself directly regulated by contact with the universal principle of being. The perfection of the creature endowed with reason, then, does not consist only in what is proper to its nature, but in whatever of supernatural perfection may be given to it by the grace of God. (IIa, IIae, 2, 3.)

This last sentence is of profound importance. It is the vision of God which will establish perfect harmony in man. In enjoyment of the one good which is capable of satisfying his desires, man will love created things with a pure love, unmixed with self-seeking, without any desire to dominate. When nothing is put in place of the absolute which is God, there will be a perfect unity in the powers of feeling and knowing, in the joy of entire submission to Father, Son and Holy Spirit. "Man's life is the vision of God", as St Irenaeus said.

THE BUILDING OF THE HUMAN COMMUNITY

The secret of the completion of human personality is a willingness to be unceasingly created by God. It is also the secret of creating the human community. Egotism, which results in the idea of the superman, kills human relationships. In the solitude of Pierre Emmanuel's Prince there is a breaking of the inner unity: "Each one found himself to be numberless, infested with grubs that bored through him" (*Babel*).

There follows a break with the world. When God is abolished there remain only sin and division, hostility and death. Where should we look for life if we shut out the author of our lives? It is the eternal drama of Adam's sin. By refusing to be dependent on God our first parent cast his descendants into disorder and death. Dostoevski felt this keenly. With the skill of genius he traces the character of the atheist, Ivan Karamazov. Ivan's tragedy is that he no longer has any contact with God, and by that very fact he is out of touch with the world. His only use for it is to get pleasure out of it and defile it. He confides his morality to his half-brother, Smerdiakov: if our souls are not immortal, if God does not exist, then anything is permissible. And so the servant kills his father. All liberty that is not from God must inevitably be turned against others. He also explains that before he was a Christian he had no idea what Christian charity demanded. When he was an officer he had once struck his orderly. Later he confessed his fault:

> I saw the scene as if it were happening all over again: the poor lad, standing in front of me while I struck his face with all my might, his hands on his trouser seams, his head erect, his eyes wide open, and trembling at every blow but not daring so much as to raise his arms to shield himself! How can a man be reduced to such state—to be beaten by another man! What a crime! It was like a needle piercing my soul. I felt as if I had lost my wits, and the sun was shining, and leaves gave cheer to one's sight, and birds were praising the Lord . . . Lord, can it be true, I thought as I wept, perhaps I am the most wicked of men, the worst there is (*The Brothers Karamazov*).

Later, when he had become the spiritual director as we know, he was to say: "We are all responsible for each other and each is guilty before the others, is convicted for them and for everything, and I myself more than the rest."

At the bottom of all this discussion is the question of a proper idea of man. Christian thought is aware of this. We know quite well that the Christian is grafted on to human nature just as God made it. The heart of the matter is primarily respect for man, for the whole man whatever he is like, without distinction of nation or race.

*   *   *

Salvation lies in the man who is saved, a man whose eyes are opened to God, and who is enabled by that very fact to set about making a new world. St Ignatius of Antioch, as we remember, longed to be rooted in the Father, the Son and the Holy Spirit, to the point of sharing their thought and action (*Epistle to the Magnesians*, 13. 1–2). The way is marked for us. We must reproduce among men the relationships we have been discovering between Father, Son and Holy Spirit. Far from making human nature into an absolute, sufficient to itself, we must pledge it to fulfil the demands of love. And the first of these is renunciation for another's sake. No one belongs to himself alone. It follows that we cannot live a truly human life if we refuse to share in the dialogue, if we take a merely selfish pleasure in what we have. A person, on this level, is a being who will sacrifice himself through renunciation in order to be completely available to God and to all that he loves. We have seen the necessity of this inclination to God. Nothing exists which does not depend on God for the satisfaction of the deepest needs of its nature. In relation to others we can guess the need, for the good of one is the good of all, no one could keep what he has if the whole community did not combine to defend his right to it. A human person must know how to sacrifice himself for all the others, but all men bear the responsibility for safeguarding the rights of each. Saint-Exupéry's pages on this subject are without equal. His writing is steeped in the nostalgia of a world in labour to bring forth the *cor unum et anima una* of the first community in the Acts of the Apostles. He describes a meal at the farm, when the farmer handed round the bread in silence. At that moment he felt himself bound to his friends with whom he was sharing it, but also, "through them, to his whole country". For the bread came from the fields round about, but how many hands were needed before it could reach the table! And besides, bread, like wheat, "is something more than mere bodily food".

"It plays so many parts! We learned to see in bread an image of the nobility of work, because it must be earned by the sweat of one's brow. We learned to see in bread the essential expression of pity, because of the bread which is given away in times of distress. The taste of bread which is shared has no equal."

Yet the farmer has not impoverished himself by distributing his bread to others. He has given nothing. He has shared and exchanged. He has made one. In this passage full of exultation Saint-Exupéry has rediscovered the oriental tradition, where people know how to share their bread with a stranger. To offer bread to a man is to offer him a share in one's work, in the life of the household. It means treating him as God's ambassador, promising him the protection of one's own roof, even though he may be an enemy. "If Zeus has sent you illfortune, O stranger, then you must submit to it, but since you are here in our city and our land, do not fear that you will lack clothing, nor anything else that should be given to a poor suppliant when we meet him." For, Homer adds, "poor or suppliant, all come to us from Zeus" (from the *Odyssey*).

Greek and Oriental respect the stranger, seeing in him a mysterious and sacred quality: *mysterious*, for his origin is unknown and he must not be questioned, he is simply the one whom God has sent: *sacred*, precisely because he is sent by God. Plato set down this rule: "With regard to strangers, we must bear in mind that agreements made with them have a peculiar holiness; for all faults committed by strangers or against them are, more than those committed between citizens, closely linked to a jealous god. In fact, isolated as he is, without companions or family, a stranger inspires more pity in both men and gods; it follows that he who has the greatest power to avenge him is the quickest to come to his aid, and he who can do so above all, at all times, is the demon or god of strangers, who follows in the train of Zeus Xenios."

This tradition of hospitality and social responsibility was not unknown in the Bible, which indeed has its own rich contribution to add. Abraham once prostrated himself before his mysterious visitors, performed for them the usual ritual ablutions, and then served them in person (Gen. 18). It is fitting to be a *servant* to the stranger whom God has sent. But this word *servant* is precisely the one that Jesus used to describe himself at the moment when he was preparing to create—in the strictest sense of the word—the community of man: "If I have washed your feet, I who am the Master and the Lord, you in your turn ought to wash each other's feet; I have been setting you an example, which will teach you in your turn to do what I have done for you. Believe me, no slave can be greater than his master, no apostle greater than he by whom he was sent. Now that you know this, blessed are you if you perform it" (John 13. 14–17).

We shall be judged by our love, so the Master tells us, because it is love that unites. To fight against love is to fight against that unity for which he prayed (Matt. 25. 31–46; John 17).

The heart that is filled with a love that serves is the future temple of peace. Contemplation is the architect which will make it rise from the ground. But love is God, and comes from God. It must be learnt from him. First of all we must imitate the Father. Like him we must create. That means to serve, not to demand service. Fatherhood in the flesh draws all its value from this interpretation. The father has a son, not for himself but so that he may give him to all. All that he keeps for himself is the fatherhood by which he was able to give himself. In his privation lies his wealth, he is more of a man when he has given his son to serve the community. The distortion of fatherhood is to be found in the bourgeois paternalism of the nineteenth century, whose final but painful contortions can be witnessed in our time. Paternalism was based on the will to power, on a superiority complex. It took up a protecting attitude in order to rule more effectively. Its aim was not to serve but to gain. It kept its inferiors in a state of tutelage so as to give more scope to its powers of directing, and if it assumed liberalism it was simply to provide an excuse for despising human rights and making them subordinate to itself. It would allow no collaboration, for fear it might be supplanted. Almsgiving took the place of justice and love.

Today we are anxious to reforge the links between human beings. The abolition of all forms of paternalism is essential for this. Only by imitating our heavenly Father can we create a true community, whether the problem be in industry, colonization or the life of the Church. No one must act in order to rule, or think that he is of such a superior nature that he has the right to make others subject to him, instead he must serve others without self-interest. The utmost care for the needs of others is essential, for that is the measure of love, as Abbé Blanchard says: "The degree of love can be measured, psychologically, by the degree of care we give to another."

It takes time, and patience and a willingness to serve instead of enjoying oneself: "What are you doing with those stars?" said the little prince to the business man.

"Nothing. I own them."

"But you are no use to the stars——" said the little prince in his dream (Saint-Exupéry).

To give as the Father does, to share his work—that is the task assigned to all paternity, and hence to all forms of apostolate. That was the longing that St Paul cherished in his inmost heart when he wrote to the Thessalonians: "We have never asked for human praise, yours or another's, although, as apostles of Christ, we might have made heavy demands on you. No, you found us innocent as babes in your company; no nursing mother ever cherished her children more; in our great longing for you, we desired nothing better than to offer you our own lives as well as God's gospel, so greatly had we learned to love you" (1 Thess. 2. 6–8).

To know, as the Son knows, as the Apostle and all the saints knew, how to receive from God and so to let ourselves be consumed in him—that is to bear the image of the Son also. "I have given them thy message. . . . I have sent them into the world on my errand. . . ." (John 17. 14, 18).

None of them sought to gain personal importance through his gift. They had only one desire—that God's fruitfulness should be acknowledged. In that same action they imitated the Spirit also, for these are the ways of love. When a man imitates the Blessed Trinity, he in his turn becomes a light, becomes a cement that binds men together to the Father's glory. On the mountain, Jesus mapped out their course clearly: "Your light must shine so brightly before men that they can see your good work, and glorify your Father who is in heaven" (Matt. 5. 16).

Then the drama of Babel will reach its climax. Once the famous tower was the seed of division because it was nothing but the fruit of pride and the desire to dominate—God must be dethroned at whatever cost. But each man, like the most utterly damned in Dante's hell, found himself in a horrifying frozen solitude. Love gives birth to a better world, Eden recovered and the days in Paradise renewed:

In the days when men spoke the same tongue and the same words,
In the days when God enveloped their thoughts like a seamless tent,
When the centre was everywhere, the sea enclosed in a single heart;
None thought of building towns, of mortaring men together like
      stone upon stone,
Each man found in his brother's eyes his value and his home.
They were free. Their fatherland flowed in their bloodstream.
Each was the orchard, each one gave and got, knowing nothing
      of mine and thine,
For their likeness flowed from their spring,
Whence one love in all found wonder in each man's otherness.
                                        (Pierre Emmanuel, *Babel*.)

For, as Jesus said, "It is more blessed to give than to receive" (Acts 20. 35).

The joy of enriching another, and making him fruitful—that is the joy of the Father who begets and gives his Son, that is the joy of the Son who is the revelation of the Father, he whose prayer obtained for us the gift of the Spirit. That is the joy of being, like the Holy Spirit, a love that is first passive but afterwards praise of Father and Son. To make a complete gift of self, in imitation of the Blessed Trinity—that is the only way to create, as God creates in himself, a true community.

SELECT BIBLIOGRAPHY

SCHEEBEN, Mathias J.: *Mysteries of Christianity*, London and St Louis, Herder, 1946.

LEBRETON, Jules, S.J.: *The Life and Teaching of Jesus Christ*, London, Burns Oates, and New York, Macmillan, 1958.

SHEED, F. J.: *Theology and Sanity*, London and New York, Sheed and Ward, 1947.

BERNADOT, M. V., O.P.: *From Holy Communion to the Blessed Trinity*, London, Sands, 1934, and Westminster, Md, Newman Press, 1947.

HENRY, A. M., O.P.: *God and his Creation*, Volume 2 in the Theology Library; Cork, Mercier Press, and Chicago, Fides, 1956.

The Twentieth Century Encyclopedia of Catholicism

The number of each volume indicates its place in the over-all series and not the order of publication.

All titles are subject to change.

DATE DUE

JAN 6 '91			